Talk about Books!

Talk about Books!

A Guide for Book Clubs, Literature Circles, and Discussion Groups, Grades 4–8

Elizabeth Knowles and Martha Smith

LIBRARIES

UNLIMITED

A Member of the Greenwood Publishing Group

Westport, Connecticut • London

Library of Congress Cataloging-in-Publication Data

Knowles, Elizabeth, 1946–
    Talk about books! : a guide for book clubs, literature circles, and
discussion groups, grades 4–8 / by Elizabeth Knowles and Martha Smith.
        p.   cm.
    Includes bibliographical references and index.
    ISBN 1–59158–023–4 (alk. paper)
        1. Group reading. 2. Reading (Elementary) 3. Children—Books and reading.
I. Smith, Martha, 1946– II. Title.
    LC6631.K56   2003
    372.41 ′62—dc21   2003051582

British Library Cataloguing in Publication Data is available.

Library of Congress Catalog Card Number: 2003051582
ISBN: 1–59158–023–4

First published in 2003

Libraries Unlimited, 88 Post Road West, Westport, CT 06881
A Member of Greenwood Publishing Group, Inc.
www.lu.com

Printed in the United States of America

∞

The paper used in this book complies with the
Permanent Paper Standard issued by the National
Information Standards Organization (Z39.48–1984).

10 9 8 7 6 5 4 3 2 1

Copyright Acknowledgments

Photo of Carl Dueker: Photo of Carl Dueker reprinted by permission of Houghton
Mifflin Children's Books.
Photo of Jan Greenberg: Reprinted with permission.
Photo of Margaret Peterson Haddix: Reprinted with permission.
Photo of Diane Stanley: Reprinted with permission.

Contents

Introduction

Book clubs can take many forms. They can be conducted by a classroom teacher within the school day as part of the language arts program. They can include students from more than one grade level. They can be an after-school activity. They can be conducted by the media specialist, alone or with classroom teachers, at the school's library media center. Book clubs can include the students and their parents and/or grandparents. They can be after school, in the evening, or on a Saturday morning. Use this book as a resource for book clubs.

Any way you put them together, book clubs are a fun way to share literature, discover an author, or read by a theme. The idea is to encourage thoughtful discussion about a book rather than assigning skill sheets and literal comprehension questions. When implemented in the classroom as part of the literature program, book clubs include reading, writing, instruction, and class-sharing time. The emphasis is on discussion rather than comprehension questions, reading response journals rather than worksheets, and speaking and listening rather than seatwork. The entire class should also get together to discuss common issues and themes from books they have read.

This book can also be a resource for literature circles, as it promotes reading and fosters literary discussion. Daniels (1994) states that using literature circles is a reading strategy that combines the principles of cooperative learning, independent reading, and group discussion. It is important in helping students become life-long readers. The power of collaborative grouping is well documented. Collaborative learning has been defined as a key ingredient of best educational practice. It is open-ended and student-centered, and the limited size of the groups compels each member to be an active participant and a responsible group member.

Research also shows that independent reading is the single factor most strongly associated with reading achievement. Students who choose books for themselves and read on their own become the strongest readers.

Daniels (1994) also points out that literature circles manifest most or all of these key features:

• Students choose their own reading materials.
• Small temporary groups are formed, based on book choice.
• Different groups read different books.
• Groups meet on a regular schedule to discuss their reading.

- Students take notes to guide them in their reading and discussion.
- Discussion topics come from the students.
- Group meetings aim to be open, natural conversations about books, so personal connections, digressions, and open-ended questions are welcome.
- In newly formed groups, students play a rotating assortment of task roles.
- The teacher serves as a facilitator, not as a group member or instructor.
- Evaluation is by teacher observation and student self/group evaluation.
- When books are finished, readers share with their classmates and then new groups are formed around new reading choices.

Rosenblatt (1978) states that reading is a transaction, a two-way process between the reader and the text at a special time and with certain circumstances. What each reader brings to the reading can affect the connection or outcome.

In literature circles, discussions follow individual responses or reactions to the reading. The discussions are not based on answering teacher-directed questions, according to Langer (1995).

Calkins (2000) thinks teachers feel guilty if their students are spending a class period free-reading. Teachers somehow feel they are not teaching if they allow students to make their own choices and find their own meaning in what they read.

Daniels (1994) also feels that because of the focus on testing, teachers do not feel comfortable with the kinds of assessment associated with literature circles. The tools of kidwatching, narrative observational logs, checklists, student conferences, and group interviews are the evaluation equipment. In literature circles, teachers require students to take responsibility for their own book selections, topic choices, role sheets, reading assignments, record-keeping, and self and group evaluations.

Noe and Johnson (1999) claim that when readers discuss insights, raise questions, cite related experiences, and wonder about or puzzle over situations prompted by what they read, literature takes on a new life. Interpretation is dynamic, but it is limited when we read alone. When we provide students with a place to discuss their own interpretations and listen to other readers add their interpretations, a book becomes even more meaningful. Rather than passively waiting for others to impose questions and assign worksheets, students involved in discussion raise their own questions and consider their own experiences.

Group discussions are an important element of literature circles. To foster discussion, quality open-ended questions are necessary. We have included open-ended discussion questions in each chapter.

Knowles and Smith (2001) discuss the ways to acquire books for book clubs and literature circles. The following ideas were used to enhance our library and classroom collections.

Library Gift Book Program

At the beginning of the school year, send or hand out a general flyer explaining the program to all parents. Interested parents make a specified donation to the library, and the person honored is the first to take out the gift book. The funds generated cover the cost of the entire program, including preselected books and stationery. A bookplate is placed in the book to mark the occasion. The honored person is given a bookmark inscribed with his or her name and the occasion as a reminder of the donated book.

Possible gift book suggestions are numerous. We have even had a book donated in honor of a new family member—a puppy! Following are some suggestions:

> In Memory Of
> Have a Great School Year
> Congratulations on a Good Year
> Happy Valentines Day—I love you! (a small red heart was affixed to the book-plate and bookmark)
> To a Special Teacher
> Merry Christmas
> Happy Hanukkah

This is a very successful program. Solicit two or three reliable parents from the parents' association to organize and supervise the mailings and paperwork.

Bookshare Book Fair

The Bookshare Book Fair runs like any other book fair with the exception that students and parents provide the books sold. Three weeks prior to the book fair, students bring in books they no longer want or have outgrown. Books are sorted by age group and checked for appropriateness. All books are sold for 50 cents each, regardless of whether they are paperback or hardcover. The book fair is held in the library with the understanding that the library staff may select those books which would enhance the school's collection.

We hold this function twice a year, once in the fall and once in the spring. The biggest problem we have is the storage of books prior to the book fair. Because we tended to receive a large number of books for the very young child, we invited the local nursery schools to come and buy on the last day of the book fair. Unsold books were either saved for the next book fair or donated to appropriate local charities. This worthwhile program enhanced the library's collection and placed recycled books in the hands of many, many children.

School Book Clubs

School book clubs are another source of books and are worth the record-keeping. They are a source of less expensive books. If you are concerned that some of your children are unable to purchase books, try using your bonus points for extra books. Book clubs are a good source for multiple copies of a particular book or a set of books related to one of the sessions.

Civic Organizations

Identify community sponsors and civic groups for grant money or donations. Some organizations to consider are Kiwanis, Junior League, Rotary, public libraries, local businesses, neighborhood associations, and your school's parents' association. A letter or a personal visit from the moderators might be most effective. Let the organization know their support will be gratefully acknowledged on all handouts.

How to Use This Book

If you are a classroom teacher who will use these ideas in a language arts program, this book supplies you with all the information you will need. You'll find author information, Web sites about the authors, and author contact information. There are suggestions for connecting the theme to content areas with various activities. These are merely suggestions: take the basic ideas and expand them according to your students' needs, your curriculum, your current focus, and so on.

Each chapter includes Web sites for more information on the theme. As always with Web sites, please check them before giving them to students. Web sites can be here today and gone tomorrow, they can suddenly display offensive or questionable ad banners, and their content can change.

Bibliographies of titles, some annotated, can give your students more to read by the focus author or on the theme. We have provided lists of teacher resources where books were available. Some themes include Web sites for teachers. Some of the teacher resources have older publication dates but are still available. We have even included suggestions for story-related snacks.

If you are planning to do your book club as an after-school activity, at a library, or with parents, there are some things to remember. You need to select a convenient time. If you are including parents, your parents' organization might be able to help you select a time, and they might also assist you in notifying the parents. You might include meeting dates in a school or grade-level newsletter, on the school's Web site, and on the school's or library's master calendar. In all cases you should make sure you adapt the suggestions in the book to your particular group or situation. You might want to provide name tags and you might want to break a large group into smaller groups for discussion time. You might also want to post some guidelines such as the following for effective discussions:

- Respect the opinions and ideas of others.
- Take turns sharing thoughts.
- Keep your comments brief and to the point.
- Be prepared—if you have a portion of the book to read, please do so.
- Speak clearly and loudly enough so others in your group can hear.
- Participate and have fun!

1

Night Hoops by Carl Deuker
(Houghton Mifflin Company, 2000)

Genre: Sports Novel
Theme: Basketball

Introduction

This book club will have the most meaning if it is done in the spring when the NBA team schedules are winding down and excitement is heating up for the playoffs. Basketball will be featured in the news, in magazines, and in stores. *Night Hoops* is the perfect title to read and discuss. Carl Deuker has written several sports novels. This theme includes lots of interesting Web sites and content area activities, all related to basketball, and a list of titles, some annotated, with basketball as the theme.

Summary of *Night Hoops*

Nick Abbott and Trent Dawson have nothing in common but basketball. Or so it seems. As the basketball season progresses, their lives become unexpectedly intertwined. In this story of an unlikely bond, award-winning author Carl Deuker explores that dark and confusing place between loneliness and friendship, between faithfulness and betrayal. Filled with gripping game play, the novel will leave readers wondering how much they themselves would reach out to a kid like Trent.

Information About Carl Deuker

Carl Deuker was born on October 26, 1950 in San Francisco. He received a B.A. in 1972 from the University of California at Berkeley and an M.A. from the University of Washington. He was never really an athlete; he did make a few teams, but most often he was a spectator. Between the ages of eight and twelve, he played imaginary games that eventually served as the groundwork for his writing. In 1992, he won the South Carolina Young Adult Book Award for *On the Devil's Court*.

Carl Deuker has taught in schools for over twenty years and lives in Seattle with his wife and young daughter. He has written several sports novels, three of which, *On the Devil's Court, Heart of a Champion, and Painting the Black,* were selected as ALA Best Books for Young Adults.

Discussion Questions

- Can you imagine what it would be like to have a parent favor a sibling over you?
- When serious family issues are involved, is it difficult to compromise?
- Is it easy to make choices? How did making choices affect this story?
- Is it important to have a teacher who cares about you?
- What similarities and differences did you see between Nick's and Trent's older brothers?
- Do any of the events in the book relate to your life?
- What did you like/dislike about this book?
- With which character did you connect?
- What would you have done if you were part of the story and you could have helped a character?
- Were there any twists and turns in the story that surprised you?

Content Area Connections

Math

Students may: Work in groups to create math problems for their classmates, using basketball statistics.

- Compare the salaries of some of the top professional players.
- Calculate shooting percentages or points-per-game averages.
- Find the dimensions of an NBA court and determine the area and perimeter of the court as well as the area of the center circle and the free-throw circle.
- Which NBA team has the best winning percentage in the current year?

Writing

Students may:

- Create a brochure about their favorite professional or college team or player.
- Use different poetic forms—diamante, cinquain, couplets, ballads—to write poems about basketball or a favorite player.
- Write a biography of James Naismith.

Social Studies

Students may:

- Find out how basketball was started and if it has changed since then. Who was the first person credited with starting the game of basketball and when? Make a chart or a poster with their findings.
- Track their favorite team from city to city as they compete during the season. Make a chart and calculate and record the miles they travel from city to city and record the weather highlights at each stop.
- Find out about basketball in the Olympics. Which countries have teams? Are there women's teams? What year were professional basketball players first allowed to play?

Science

Students may:

- Find out what makes a basketball bounce. See http://www.physicscentral. com/lou/lou-02-01.html.
- Consider all the angles and determine the best angle for making a three-point shot.

Technology

Students may:

- Search the Internet to find statistics about their favorite team or player.
- Go to http://www.hoophall.com/history/history.htm and find James Naismith's Original 13 Basketball Rules and tell how these rules have changed. Create a PowerPoint presentation or a large chart on poster board to show the changes.

Physical Education

- Get the PE teachers involved by asking them to spend some time specifically on basketball skills and rules. Ask them to teach games that help the students develop specific skills.

- This Web site is a great place to look for basketball-related games: http://pe.central.vt.edu/.

Mapping

Students may:

- Create a concept map about basketball. Put basketball in the center with history, favorite teams, favorite players, and important statistics in the second row.

    Snack: Sports drinks, power bars
    Decorations: NBA posters, team T-shirts, books about professional basketball stars, team banners

Annotated Titles About Basketball

Bennett, James W. *Blue Star Rapture.* Simon & Schuster Books for Young Readers, 1998.

T.J. pretended to help Tyrone and in doing so he felt important. Coaches knew T.J. looked out for the big guy, Tyrone, and asked him to encourage Tyrone and keep track of any of his communications with scouts for colleges. After the two of them go to Full Court, a basketball camp, T.J. realizes he is a work in transition. In the future he is out of the loop with Tyrone. T.J. is a good player in his own way and needs to perfect himself. Mature language.

Burleigh, Robert. *Hoops.* Harcourt Brace and Company, 1997.

This is a picture book for all the players who have ever felt hot asphalt burn beneath their shoes, danced a cat-footed dance along a baseline, or heard the sound of a basketball sink through a hoop catching nothing but air!

Christopher, Matt. *Johnny Long Legs.* Little, Brown, 1970.

Johnny's mother remarried and they moved from New York City to a smaller town to live with his new stepfather and stepbrother. At Johnny's new school, the basketball team expects him to jump higher than anyone else because of his long legs. When he can't, the coach tells him to walk, run, and jump all he can. Will that be enough?

Coy, John. *Strong to the Hoop.* Lee & Low, 1999.

This picture book captures the competition between the skins and the shirts on the local basketball court. Ten-year-old James will get his chance to play when Luke sprains his ankle. The mixed-media images of photography and photo collages are an interesting combination.

Macy, Sue, ed. *Girls Got Game.* Henry Holt and Company, 2001.

Sue Macy has collected nine original stories and poems for middle school and young adult girls. Sue Macy grew up in the era when one girl out of twenty-seven participated in high school sports. Today it's one girl out of three. These stories and poems will demonstrate to girls that through athletics they are able to develop their physical and emotional well-being, which will help them manage life's challenges.

Myers, Walter Dean. *Slam!* Scholastic Incorporated, 1996.
Greg Harris transferred from Carver High School in his neighborhood to Latimer Arts Magnet School. Latimer was entering its fifth losing season in basketball. Greg—Slam—has all the right moves on the basketball court, but he has to prove to his present coach that he is a team player. Slam has the year to figure out his life, his future, his girlfriend, his studies, and his best friend, Ice.

———. *The Outside Shot.* Laurel-Leaf Books, 1984.
Harlem is the only place Lonnie Jackson has ever lived and now he has one year to keep it together and make it in a Midwestern college in Indiana.

Smith, Charles R., Jr. *Rimshots, Basketball Pix, Rolls, and Rhythms.* Dutton Children's Books, 1999.
Charles Smith combines basketball poetry and stories with duotone photographs. His table of contents includes I Remember, Please Put Me In, Coach, and Everything I Need to Know in Life, I Learned from Basketball.

Soto, Gary. *Taking Sides.* Harcourt Brace Jovanovich, 1991.
Lincoln Mendoza is in the eighth grade and a star basketball player newly moved ten miles north to a better neighborhood. Next Tuesday the two rival schools will be playing each other. Lincoln misses his old school with its black, brown, and yellow faces. He knows he will feel like a traitor when he faces them the next time.

Additional Titles About Basketball

Adoff, Arnold. *The Basket Counts.* Simon & Schuster Books for Young Readers, 2000.
Anderson, Joan. *Rookie: Tamika Whitmore's First Year in the WNBA.* Penguin Putnam Books for Young Readers, 2000.
Bird, Larry. *Drive: The Story of My Life.* Doubleday, 1989.
Brooks, Bruce. *The Moves Make the Man.* Harper & Row, 1984.
———. *Prince.* HarperCollins, 1998.
Christopher, Matt. *Wheel Wizards: It's a Whole New Ballgame for Seth.* Little, Brown, 2000.
———. *Center Court Sting.* Little, Brown, 1998.
Cooper, Ilene. *Choosing Sides.* HarperCollins Children's Book Group, 1990.
Crutcher, Chris. *Chinese Handcuffs.* HarperCollins Children's Book Group, 1989.
Dygard, Thomas J. *Tournament Upstart.* Morrow Avon, 1998.
———. *The Rebounder.* Morrow Avon, 1994.
———. *Outside Shooter.* Morrow Avon, 1998.

———. *Rebound Caper.* Penguin Putnam Books for Young Readers, 1992.

Gutman, Dan. *The Million Dollar Shot.* Hyperion Books for Children, 1997.

Holdsclaw, Chamique. *Chamique! On Family, Focus, and Basketball.* Scribner, 2000.

Hoopmania: The Book of Basketball History and Trivia. Rosen Publishing Group, 2002.

Jordan, Deloris and Roslyn. *Salt in His Shoes: Michael Jordan in Pursuit of a Dream.* Simon & Schuster Children's Publishing, 2002.

Klass, David. *Danger Zone.* Scholastic Incorporated, 1996.

Lannin, Joanne. *A History of Basketball for Girls and Women: From Bloomers to Big Leagues.* Lerner Publishing Group, 2000.

Revoyr, Nina. *The Necessary Hunger.* Simon & Schuster, 1997.

Russo, Marisa. *House of Sports.* HarperCollins Children's Book Group, 2002.

Savage, Jeff. *Kobe Bryant: Basketball Big Shot.* Lerner Publishing Group, 2001.

Smith, Pohla and Steve Wilson. *Shaquille O'Neal: Superhero at Center.* Rosen Publishing Group, 2002.

Sweeney, Joyce. *Players.* Winslow Press, 2000.

Ultimate Sports: Short Stories by Outstanding Writers for Young Adults. Bantam Doubleday Dell Books for Young Readers, 1995.

Wallace, Rich. *Playing Without the Ball: A Novel in Four Quarters.* Alfred A. Knopf Books for Young Readers, 2000.

Weesner, Theodore. *Winning the City.* Summit Books, 1990.

Annotated Titles by Carl Deuker

Heart of a Champion. Little, Brown, 1993.
When Jimmy, who is both a baseball champion and something of an irresponsible fool, is kicked off the team, Seth faces a strain on their friendship.

On the Devil's Court. Little, Brown, 1989.
Struggling with his feelings of inadequacy and his failure to make the basketball team in his new school, seventeen-year-old Joe Faust finds himself willing to trade his soul for one perfect season of basketball.

Painting the Black. Houghton Mifflin Company, 1997.
When star athlete Josh Daniels moves in across the street, Remy Ward doesn't realize how much his life will change during his senior year at Seattle's Crown Hill High.

Teacher Resource About Basketball

Smith, Robert. *Thematic Unit: Basketball.* Teacher Created Materials, 2002.

Web Sites About Basketball

Kids Zone Basketball
http://cbs.sportsline.com/u/kidszone/basketball/
Basketball Mania
http://tqjunior.thinkquest.org/3952/
Harlem Globetrotters
http://www.harlemglobetrotters.com/
Junior NBA
http://www.nba.com/jrnba/
Hoop Hall History Page
http://www.hoophall.com/history/history.htm
Fact Monster—Basketball
http://www.factmonster.com/ipka/A0882905.html

Web Sites About Carl Deuker

Bulletin of The Center for Children's Books: Carl Deuker
http://alexia.lis.uiuc.edu/puboff/bccb/0997feat.html
Interview with Carl Deuker on Amazon.com
http://www.amazon.com/exec/obidos/show-interview/d-c-eukerarl/
103–0985017–1568642

Contact Publisher:

Houghton Mifflin Children's Books, 8th Floor
222 Berkeley Street
Boston, MA 02116-3764

2

Heart to Heart: New Poems Inspired by Twentieth-Century American Art edited by Jan Greenberg (Harry N. Abrams, Incorporated, Publishers, 2001)

Genre: Poetry
Theme: Poetry and Art

Introduction

This is a good book club for February, mainly because the focus book, *Heart to Heart,* is filled with heartwarming poems and artwork. Jan Greenberg has organized a beautiful collection of poems and corresponding artwork. Students should be encouraged to create a similar collection for their own class book or bulletin board display. The activities focus on using poetic forms and looking at other titles where poetry and art are similarly connected. The Web sites provide creative information about poetry and excellent information on the focus author, Jan Greenberg.

Summary of *Heart to Heart*

This book is a celebration of the creative interplay between poetry and art. Young readers can explore the connections between these two art forms within the context of America in the twentieth century. Forty-three contemporary poets each selected a work of art—a painting, sculpture, or photograph—and wrote a poem translating the visual experience into words. The result is a collection of original poems inspired by encounters with art.

Information About Jan Greenberg

Jan Greenberg lives in St. Louis, Missouri, where she grew up loving to read. "My parents' library was filled with an assortment of books ranging from Plato's *Dialogues* to *Alice in Wonderland*. It was there in that cozy room with a fireplace that I developed my eclectic tastes in literature."

Jan's three daughters, Lynne, Jeanne, and Jackie, influenced her decision to write for young readers. "Teenagers are the most interesting people I know. There is no other period in one's life when certain emotions—joy, sadness, or anger—seem so intense. Now that my own children are grown, I receive wonderful ideas from young readers across the country. Of course I can still draw on autobiographical material."

Her work in art education, her conversations with artists, and her love of "looking at art" formed the basis of her recent books about American art and architecture. She enjoys traveling around the country interviewing artists, hearing their stories, and making connections between their lives and their work.

"A book is never a figment of imagination," she says. "It begins as a stomachache, a slight quiver of discomfort. It's like falling in and out of love. If the feeling is strong enough, a book may evolve. Or maybe not. But when something happens and a year later I'm holding a new book in my hand, I want to jump up and down, throw confetti, and stop everyone on the street, and say, 'Look what I've done!'"

Discussion Questions

- How do poetry and art complement each other?
- Why was the book given this title?
- What do the poetic forms have to say about the matching paintings?
- How does the way the book is organized add to the focus of the book?
- Select one of the paintings to look at closely—what mood does it create?

- What did you learn from this book?
- What did you like best about this book? Have you read any similar books?
- After reading this book, did you have different feelings from when you first began the book?
- What are your feelings about writing poetry, especially poetry prompted by artwork?
- Did you look at the brief biographies of the poets and artists? If so, did you recognize any names from other things you have read?

Content Area Connections

Language Arts

- Take a closer look at the various poetic forms used in the book. Select a poetic form and a topic and ask each student to create a poem. Compare the feelings and approaches taken by each student.
- Look at some of the other titles in the list of additional titles and review the other topics—America, African Americans, and so on. Create something similar on a topic that interests you.

Art

Students may:

- Create their own *Heart to Heart* book. Half of the students can do the artwork and the other half can create the matching poems.

Social Studies

- Some of the paintings come from specific time periods. Have the students identify the time period and see if the painting reflects the mood created by the happenings of that time.

Technology

Students may:

- Research online some of the artists and poets found in this book, and create a list of links for their classmates to explore about each one. Create a bookmark or a poster with the URLs.

Mapping

Students may:

- Make two circles—one for artists and one for poets. Create a map of those from the book and research to add more titles of poems and artwork for each.

Snack: Heart candies, cookies, red punch

Annotated Titles About Poetry and Art

Brenner, Barbara. *Voices: Poetry and Art from Around the World.* National Geographic Society, 2000.

The author has compiled traditional and contemporary poetry and art to convey the feelings of each unique continent and the people who live there.

Carle, Eric. *Eric Carle's Dragons & Other Creatures That Never Were.* Philomel Books, 1991.

Eric Carle created mythological and legendary creatures to illustrate poetry from many authors, such as Karla Kuskin, X.J. Kennedy, Myra Cohn Livingston, and Paul Fleishman.

Cummings, Pat. *Talking with Artists: Volume Three.* Clarion Books, 1999.

After a brief introductory interview with the thirteen children's illustrators, the editor asks the same questions as she did in the previous volumes. Secret Techniques and five of the illustrators' favorite books are included at the end.

Demi. *Demi's Secret Garden: Poems Compiled and Illustrated by Demi.* Henry Holt and Company, 1993.

Includes twenty children's poems richly illustrated by Demi with some of the artworks spanning across foldout pages.

Florian, Douglas. *Insectlopedia.* Harcourt, 1998.

This book includes twenty-one short poems and accompanying paintings about a variety of insects, such as the hornet, walking stick, io moth, and inchworm.

Joyce, William. *The World of William Joyce Scrapbook: Text and Art by William Joyce.* HarperCollins, 1997.

This cleverly designed book is a biography of William Joyce told with photographs and his illustrations. He briefly talks about some of his children's books and what inspired him to write them and also previews four new books.

Krull, Kathleen. *Lives of the Artists: Masterpieces, Messes, (and What the Neighbors Thought).* Harcourt Brace & Company, 1995.

This book includes the interesting lives of twenty artists and their neighbors' reactions. Includes Andy Warhol, Salvador Dali, Georgia O'Keeffe, Pablo Picasso, and Leonardo da Vinci.

———. *Lives of the Writers: Comedies, Tragedies (and What the Neighbors Thought).* Harcourt Brace & Company, 1994.

Brief biographies of twenty writers with the details that make their lives memorable. Some are as follows: Miguel De Cervantes, William Shakespeare, Edgar Allan Poe, Charlotte and Emily Bronte, Emily Dickinson, Robert Louis Stevenson, Carl Sandburg, and Langston Hughes.

Longfellow, Henry Wadsworth. *The Midnight Ride of Paul Revere.* Handprint Books, 2001.

Christopher Bing won the Caldecott Honor Award for his first book, *Casey at the Bat.* This book is too good to be missed, a beautifully designed and illustrated rendition of another famous poem.

Nelson, Marilyn. *Carver: A Life in Poems.* Front Street, 2001.
This award-winning book uses poems to tell the story of the life of George Washington Carver: slave, botanist, inventor, painter, musician, and teacher. It won these awards: Coretta Scott King Honor, John Newbery Honor, National Book Award Finalist, and Boston Globe-Horn Book Award.

Nye, Naomi Shihab. *The Space Between Our Footsteps: Poems and Paintings from the Middle East.* Simon & Schuster Books for Young Readers, 1998.
The Greek word anthology means gathering of flowers. Naomi Nye has brought together not flowers but poetry combined with full-color paintings from writers and painters of the Middle East in this special book. Notes about the contributors are included.

Panzer, Nora, ed. *Celebrate America in Poetry and Art.* Hyperion Press, 1999.
This book includes paintings, sculpture, drawings, and photographs from the National Museum of American Art at the Smithsonian. It is divided into five sections: the country's landscape, its melting-pot makeup, city and rural life, American history, and American pastimes. Writers and illustrators include Maya Angelou, Robert Frost, Winslow Homer, and Thomas Hart Benton, to name a few.

Rochelle, Belinda, ed. *Words with Wings: A Treasury of African-American Poetry and Art.* HarperCollins, 2000.
Twenty poems by distinguished African American poets are paired with twenty works of art by acclaimed African American artists. The themes are varied: work, pain, love, anger, regret, joy, and sorrow. The artwork is colorful and the poems will touch your heart and dazzle your eyes. Notes about each of the artists and poets are included.

Rohmer, Harriet, ed. *Just Like Me: Self-Portraits and Stories.* Children's Book Press, 1997.
Fourteen artists from many different backgrounds are highlighted in this collection. They have all created multicultural picture books for children, published by Children's Book Press. Two pages are devoted to each artist, a self-portrait on one page and a personal story on the opposite page. The artists express their concerns and feelings and reflect on what art means to them.

Additional Titles About Poetry and Art

Adoff, Arnold. *The Basket Counts.* Simon & Schuster Books for Young Readers, 2000.
Asch, Frank. *Song of the North.* Harcourt Brace and Company, 1999.
Begay, Shonto. *Navajo: Visions and Voices from Across the Mesa.* Scholastic Incorporated, 1995.
Clinton, Catherine. *I, Too, Sing America: Three Centuries of African American Poetry.* Houghton Mifflin Company, 1998.
Feelings, Tom. *Soul Looks Back in Wonder.* Puffin Books, 1993.
Heard, Georgi. *Songs of Myself: An Anthology of Poems and Art.* Mondo Publishing, 2000.

Hopkins, Lee Bennett. *My America: A Poetry Atlas of the United States.* Simon & Schuster Books for Young Readers, 2000.

———. *Hand in Hand: An American History Through Poetry.* Simon & Schuster Books for Young Readers, 1994.

Hughes, Langston. *The Block: Poems.* Viking Press, 1995.

Janeczko, Paul. *Stone Bench in an Empty Park.* Orchard Books, 2000.

Jeffers, Susan. *Brother Eagle, Sister Sky.* Dial Books, 1991.

Lach, William, ed. *Curious Cats: In Art and Poetry.* Atheneum Books for Young Readers, 1999.

Richardson, Joy. *Looking at Pictures: An Introduction to Art for Young People.* Harry N. Abrams, Inc., 1997.

Rosenberg, Liz, ed. *The Invisible Ladder: An Anthology of Contemporary American Poems for Young Readers with the Poets' Own Photos and Commentary.* Henry Holt and Company, 1996.

Sullivan, Charles. *Here Is My Kingdom: Hispanic-American Literature and Art for Young People.* Harry N. Abrams, Inc., 1994.

When the Rain Sings: Poems by Young Native Americans (by National Museum of the American Indian, Smithsonian Institution). Simon & Schuster Books for Young Readers, 1999.

Whipple, Laura, ed. *Celebrating America: A Collection of Poems and Images of the American Spirit, Poetry Compiled by Laura Whipple; Art Provided by the Art Institute of Chicago.* Philomel Books, 1994.

White, Lee. *Poetry 4 Ya Mind: A Collection of Poetry and Artwork from Getting Ready.* Northwest Media, Inc., 1999.

Yolen, Jane. *Color Me a Rhyme: Nature Poems for Young People.* Boyds Mills Press, 2000.

———. *Sacred Places.* Harcourt Brace and Company, 1996.

Annotated Titles by Jan Greenberg

With Sandra Jordan. *The American Eye: Eleven Artists of the Twentieth Century.* Delacorte Press, 1995.

The authors look at the lives of eleven artists from birth to death and their influences on America in the modern world. Discussion of the artists' work is included in the narrative. Includes a glossary of terms, a list of artworks, explanation of where to find works by the artists, and a bibliography of resources.

———. *Chuck Close Up Close.* DK Publishing, Inc., 1998.

Chuck Close overcame severe learning disabilities as a child growing up in the 1940s. His struggles with learning helped him later in life with his "larger than life portraits" and partial paralysis.

——. *Frank O. Gehry: Outside In.* Dorling Kindersley, 2000.

When Frank Gehry was only ten years old, a handwriting reader predicted he would be a famous architect. Frank switched from art classes to architecture while in school in California. Gehry likes to use materials that others would throw away. In 1997 Gehry built the Guggenheim Museum in Bilboa, Spain, with titanium walls, "an instant landmark."

——. *The Sculptor's Eye.* Delacorte Press, 1993.

The authors introduce contemporary sculpture by using examples from post World War II to familiarize the reader with the language of art. The book focuses on three questions: "What makes it a sculpture? What kinds of artistic skills are involved? What does it mean?"

——. *Vincent van Gogh: Portrait of an Artist.* Delacorte Press, 2001.

Vincent van Gogh began painting at twenty-seven and ended ten years later when he took his own life after a tortured journey. The book includes a glossary of artists, terms, and museum locations of his work.

Teacher Resources About Poetry and Art

Bonica, Diane. *Writing and Art Go Hand in Hand to Teach Language Skills.* Incentive Publications, 1988.

Classroom Technologies. *Writing and Reading Poetry: Grades 5–8.* Vision Technology in Education, 2000.

Katz, Bobbi. *American History Poems.* Scholastic Trade, 1999.

Moore, Jo Ellen and Joy Evans. *Writing Poetry with Children.* Evan-Moor Educational Publishers, 1988.

Web Sites About Poetry and Art

Giggle Poetry
http://www.gigglepoetry.com/
Magnetic Poetry
http://home.freeuk.net/elloughton13/scramble.htm
Learn to Write Poetry from Real Poets
http://teacher.scholastic.com/writewit/poetry/index.htm
Poetry Game
http://www.abc.net.au/splatt/games/poetry/default.htm
The Bulletin of the Center for Children's Books: True Blue—Jan Greenberg and Sandra Jordan
http://alexia.lis.uiuc.edu/puboff/bccb/0900true.html
The Teachers' Corner
http://www.theteacherscorner.net/writing/poetry/index.htm

Web Sites About Jan Greenberg

Jan Greenberg
http://alexia.lis.uiuc.edu/puboff/bccb/0900true.html
Meet the Author: Jan Greenberg and Sandra Johnson
http://www.eduplace.com/kids/hmr/mtai/greenberg_jordan.html
Jan Greenberg
http://authors.missouri.org/e-h/greenberg-j.html

Contact Publisher:

Harry N. Abrams, Inc.
100 Fifth Avenue
New York, NY 10011

Jan Greenberg
3 Brentmoor Park
St. Louis, MO 63105-3003
www.abramsbooks.com

3

Flipped by Wendelin Van Draanen
(Alfred A. Knopf, 2001)

Genre: Realistic Fiction
Theme: Relationships and Friendships

Introduction

Fostering friendships and good relationships both in and out of school has become more important than ever. Friendships and getting along are appropriate topics at any time. Van Draanen's book conveys the story of a relationship between a boy and girl and deals with issues most students face. The activities deal with making friends and encouraging students to widen their circles of friends. The bibliography of titles, some annotated, provides a wide variety of great stories about young people and their struggles with friendships and relationships. The Web sites include information about the focus author, Wendelin Van Draanen.

Summary of *Flipped*

The same story is told first from the viewpoint of Bryce and then from the viewpoint of Juli. It all starts when Bryce moves into the neighborhood and Juli anxiously awaits his arrival. Bryce's father immediately thinks Juli is a pest, and Bryce agrees. Bryce does everything to avoid Juli. Juli is not afraid to speak her mind and sits in a beloved sycamore tree when the owner tries to cut it down. After Juli appears in the paper supporting her cause, Bryce's grandfather becomes interested in her because Juli reminds him of his deceased wife. Bryce begins to look at Juli in a new way at the same time Juli sees through the shallowness of Bryce. Both grow in their own way, and the journey is delightful.

Information About Wendelin Van Draanen

Wendelin Van Draanen is the winner of the 1999 Edgar Allan Poe Award for Best Children's Mystery Book for *Sammy Keyes and the Hotel*

17

Thief. Books have always been a part of Wendelin Van Draanen's life. Her mother taught her to read at an early age, and she has fond memories of story time with her father, when she and her brothers would cuddle up around him and listen to him read stories.

Growing up, Van Draanen was a tomboy who loved to be outside chasing down adventure. She did not decide she wanted to be an author until she was an adult. When she tried her hand at writing a screenplay about a family tragedy, she found the process cathartic and, from that experience, turned to writing novels for adults. She soon stumbled upon the joys of writing for children.

Feedback from her readers is Van Draanen's greatest reward for writing. "One girl came up to me and told me I changed her life. It doesn't get any better than that," she said. Van Draanen hopes to leave her readers with a sense that they have the ability to steer their own destinies—that individuality is a strength, and that where there's a will, there's most certainly a way.

Wendelin Van Draanen lives with her husband and two sons in California.

Discussion Questions

- What surprises happened in this book?
- Did you find yourself identifying with one of the characters? If so, which one?
- How long did it take for this whole story to take place? Was that too much or not enough?
- Have you ever taken a stand for something you believe in? If so, describe what happened.
- How would you have handled the issues Bryce and Juli dealt with in this story?
- Did you feel like part of the story or did you feel like an observer?
- Do you agree with the way the author views life and relationships in this story?
- Did you like the way the author went from one character to the other in this book?
- Would you recommend this book to a friend? Why or why not?
- What did you learn from this story?

Content Area Connections

Language Arts

Students may:

- Write a poem or an acrostic about a friend.
- Keep a journal of observations of relationships around them.

- Create a newspaper column in which they give advice to other students with questions about friendships and relationships.

Art

Students may:

- Design a new cover for the book; include title, author, author bio, story summary, and lots of colorful artwork.
- Create a poster detailing the qualities of a friend. Make it colorful and clear.

Social Studies

Students may:

- Brainstorm ideas on approaching and including kids who appear to be loners. Look at statistics about school shootings and research to see what groups have started to try to help all kids feel part of positive circles at school.

Mapping

Students may:

- Create a mind map about friends. Use colors and symbols and be creative.

Technology

Students may:

- Go to http://www.teaching.com/keypals/ and start an e-mail correspondence with a new friend (a keypal!).

Snack: Cheese and crackers, celery and peanut butter

Annotated Titles About Relationships and Friendships

Brashares, Ann. *The Sisterhood of the Traveling Pants*. Delacorte Press, 2001.
Four friends find a pair of jeans in a thrift shop and somehow the jeans magically fit each girl. The girls are going off to different places for the summer and agree to share the pants. The story follows each girl during the time the pants are in her possession, detailing all their adventures. For older teens.

Brooks, Bruce. *Dolores: Seven Stories About Her.* HarperCollins Publishers, 2002.
Stories about Dolores begin when she is seven and end when she is a young woman of sixteen. One learns about Dolores through her experiences and relationships with her brother, father, mother, classmates, and first boyfriend. One can't help but like Dolores.

Brooks, Martha. *Being with Henry.* Dorling Kindersley, 2000.
Sixteen-year old Laker was thrown out of his house after a fight with his stepfather. He takes a bus to Bemidji and spends three weeks on his own. Two days in

a row, an older man, Henry, hands him nickels and quarters. On the second day Henry returns and asks Laker if he does yard work. Laker moves in with Henry and helps around the house, attends school, and pays rent. Laker is company for Henry, whose wife died recently. Gradually Laker begins to trust Henry and his granddaughter Charlene, and they vacation at Heron Lake. Laker comes to terms with his past and has a better understanding about why his mother was never there for him.

Burgess, Melvin. *Smack.* Henry Holt and Company, 1996.
Tar is only fourteen when he leaves home to get away from his abusive stepfather. Gemma, on the other hand, leaves home because she is bored and her parents have forbidden her to be around Tar. The two find shelter with anarchists who find abandoned buildings to live in or to squat. They gradually succumb to the heroin drug scene and slowly come back. For older teens.

Holyoke, Nancy. *A Smart Girl's Guide to Boys: Surviving Crushes, Staying True to Yourself, and Other Stuff.* American Girl Library, 2001.
Advice for girls on being friends with a boy, going out in groups, dating, breaking up, and being yourself. With quizzes, tips, and cute drawings, the presentation is appealing and fun to read.

McNeal, Laura and Tom. *Crooked.* Alfred A. Knopf, 1999.
Ninth graders Clara and Amos find their lives at home in shambles as they try to develop a romance. Amos witnesses two local hoodlum brothers destroying property, and they try to silence Amos by hitting him with a baseball bat. He becomes a hero to his friends, but he is constantly threatened and terrorized by the brothers. When the brothers stalk Clara, Amos makes a gutsy attempt to save her. This book contains some rough parts, poor adult role models, and depressing family life/values, but has strong main characters.

Oates, Joyce Carol. *Big Mouth and Ugly Girl.* HarperCollins Publishers, 2002.
"Big Mouth" Matt Donaghy gets a three-day suspension when someone reports that he threatened to blow up the school if his play wasn't accepted for the arts festival. Ursula Riggs, who calls herself Ugly Girl, heard what Matt said and came to his defense despite warnings from her mother about getting involved. Matt is shut out by his former friends and begins an awkward friendship with Ugly Girl. When Matt's family decides to sue the school and his accusers, things almost get out of hand.

Randle, Kristen. *Breaking Rank.* Morrow Junior Books, 1999.
Baby has spent most of his life as a member of a group called the Clan. They wear black and are generally feared and scorned by their classmates and neighbors. He goes against the group and takes honor classes at the high school and is assigned a peer tutor: a pretty, well-liked girl named Casey. Casey helps Baby get into the mainstream at school, but this threatens the Clan and the Cribs, the popular kids who wear leather jackets. Soon the inevitable happens and choices have to be made.

Sones, Sonia. *What My Mother Doesn't Know.* Simon & Schuster Books for Young Readers, 2001.
Sophie's story is told in free verse. She is best friends with Rachel and Grace and is looking for Mr. Right. At first she thinks it is Dylan, but the more she kisses

him the less she wants to. Then she meets Chaz on the Internet. "If I could marry a font, I'd marry his." One comment too many and she switches her e-mail address. She finally meets her masked man, her Mr. Right, and he turns out to be someone she has known all along.

Spinelli, Jerry. *Stargirl.* Alfred A. Knopf, 2000.
Stargirl Caraway, a new tenth grader at an Arizona high school, was previously home-schooled. She presents a new look to her fellow students—she wears pioneer dresses and kimonos, plays the ukulele, laughs when there is nothing to laugh at, dances when there is no music and no one else is dancing, and brings a white rat named Cinnamon to school with her. Leo falls in love with her (and is named Starboy by his teasing classmates) and asks her to act normal, with upsetting results.

Woodson, Jacqueline. *If You Come Softly.* Puffin Books, 1998.
Elisha (Ellie) is in the ninth grade at Percy High School, a private school. She bumps into Jeremiah (Miah) that very first day and immediately feels there is something familiar about him. Ellie is Jewish and Miah is Black, and their first pure love is strained by the attitudes of strangers. They are both afraid of the racist attitudes of friends and family, and just as Ellie is ready to introduce Miah to her family, tragedy strikes.
The first time they are alone Miah quotes a poem his mother used to read to him (pg 112), thus the title of the book.

Young, Karen Romano. *The Beetle and Me: A Love Story.* William Morrow and Company, 1999.
Daisy Pandolfi, a high school sophomore, is working on restoring the engine of a 1957 Volkswagen Beetle. She meets Billy Hatcher in auto-shop class, and she also works with him on the stage crew for the school musical. She has a disaster with the engine and struggles to fix it without help. She learns something from Billy Hatcher in the process.

Additional Titles About Relationships and Friendships

Blume, Judy. *Here's to You, Rachel Robinson.* Orchard Books, 1993.
——. *Just As Long As We're Together.* Orchard Books, 1987.
Bode, Janet. *Trust and Betrayal: Real Life Stories of Friends and Enemies.* Delacorte Press, 1995.
Byars, Betsy. *The Pinballs.* Harper & Row, 1977.
Cole, Brock. *The Goats.* Farrar Straus Giroux, 1987.
Cormier, Robert. *The Bumblebee Flies Away.* Pantheon Books, 1983.
Crutcher, Chris. *Staying Fat for Sarah Brynes.* Greenwillow Books, 1993.
Danziger, Paula. *Snail Mail No More.* Scholastic Press, 2000.
——. *P.S. Longer Letter Later.* Scholastic Incorporated, 1998.
Deaver, Julie Reece. *Say Goodnight, Gracie.* Harper & Row, 1988.
Fenner, Carol. *Randall's Wall.* Margaret K. McElderry Books, 1991.
Fine, Anne. *Bad Dreams.* Delacorte Press, 2000.
——. *Tulip Touch: A Novel.* Little, Brown, 1997.

Frank, Lucy K. *Oy, Joy!* DK Publishing, Inc., 1999.

Franklin, Kristine L. *Nerd No More.* Candlewick Press, 1996.

Grove, Vickie. *The Crystal Garden.* Putnam Publishing Group, 1995.

———. *Reaching Dustin.* Putnam Publishing Group, 1998.

———. *The Starplace.* Putnam Publishing Group, 1999.

Hahn, Mary Downing. *Daphne's Book.* Clarion Books, 1983.

Hamilton, Virginia. *The Planet of Junior Brown.* Macmillan Publishing Company, 1971.

Hesse, Karen. *Phoenix Rising.* Henry Holt and Company, 1994.

Hite, Sid. *Cecil in Space.* Henry Holt and Company, 1999.

Holt, Kimberly Willis. *When Zachary Beaver Came to Town.* Henry Holt and Company, 1999.

Jukes, Mavis. *Planning the Impossible.* Delacorte Press, 1999.

Kimmel, Elizabeth Cody. *Visiting Miss Caples.* Dial Books for Young Readers, 2000.

Klass, Sheila Solomon. *The Uncivil War.* Holiday House, 1997.

Koss, Amy Goldman. *The Girls.* Dial Books for Young Readers, 2000.

———. *The Ashwater Experiment.* Dial Books for Young Readers, 1999.

Kurtz, Jane. *The Storyteller's Beads.* Harcourt Brace and Company, 1998.

Levy, Elizabeth. *Seventh Grade Tango.* Hyperion Books for Children, 2000.

Lynch, Chris. *Gold Dust.* HarperCollins Publishers, 2000.

Marsden, John. *Letters from the Inside.* Houghton Mifflin Company, 1994.

Mazer, Norma Fox. *Crazy Fish.* Morrow Junior Books, 1998.

———. *Out of Control.* Morrow Junior Books, 1993.

Myers, Walter Dean. *Fast Sam, Cool Clyde, and Stuff.* Viking Press, 1975.

———. *Me, Mop, and the Moondance Kid.* Delacorte Press, 1988.

Naylor, Phyllis Reynolds. *The Grooming of Alice.* Atheneum Books for Young Readers, 2000.

Paulsen, Gary. *The Schernoff Discoveries.* Delacorte Press, 1997.

Pearson, Gayle. *Don't Call It Paradise.* Atheneum Books for Young Readers, 1999.

Peck, Richard. *Remembering the Good Times.* Delacorte Press, 1985.

Perkins, Lynne Rae. *All Alone in the Universe.* Greenwillow Books, 1999.

Peters, Julie Anne. *Define Normal: A Novel.* Little, Brown, 2000.

Philbrick, W. Rodman. *Freak the Mighty.* Blue Sky Press, 1993.

———. *Max the Mighty.* Blue Sky Press, 1998.

Rochman, Rachel, ed. *Who Do You Think You Are? Stories of Friends and Enemies.* Little, Brown, 1993.

Romain, Trevor. *Cliques, Phonies & Other Baloney.* Free Spirit, 1998.

Seymour, Tres. *The Revelation of Saint Bruce.* Orchard Books, 1998.

Sleator, William. *Oddballs: Stories.* Dutton Children's Books, 1993.

Staples, Suzanne Fisher. *Dangerous Skies.* Farrar Straus Giroux, 1996.

Strasser, Todd. *Close Call.* Putnam Publishing Group, 1999

Voigt, Cynthia. *It's Not Easy Being Bad.* Atheneum Books for Young Readers, 2000.

———. *Bad Girls.* Scholastic Incorporated, 1996.

Annotated Titles by Wendelin Van Draanen

How I Survived Being a Girl. HarperCollins Juvenile Books, 1997.
Carolyn, a sixth grader, doesn't act or dress like a girl. She has strong opinions about everything. She plays stickball and digs foxholes with her brothers. When her baby sister is born, Carolyn feels better about having another girl in the family and decides that being a girl isn't so bad after all.

Sammy Keyes and the Hollywood Mummy. Alfred A. Knopf, 2000.
Sammy and her best friend, Marissa, travel to Hollywood to surprise Sammy's mother, Lady Lana, an aspiring actress. Sammy is distressed to find her mother claiming to be 25 years old, and to make matters worse, she asks Sammy to say she is her niece, not her daughter. One of Lady Lana's friends is murdered and Sammy jumps into action to find the culprit.

Sammy Keyes and the Hotel Thief. Dell Yearling, 1998.
Sammy is bored, so she takes her Grandmother's binoculars and looks at the hotel windows across the street. She sees a man with gloves moving quickly about the room and taking money out of a purse. When he looks up, he sees Sammy watching him. Then Sammy waves as if to say hello!

Sammy Keyes and the Search for Snake Eyes. Alfred A. Knopf, 2002.
Sammy is at the video arcade at the mall when a teenage girl who is being pursued by a man with snake eyes hands her a heavy shopping bag. Inside the bag, Sammy finds a baby. She tries to find the girl and fails, so she turns the baby over to the authorities. Sammy then sets out to solve the mystery.

Sammy Keyes and the Skeleton Man. Alfred A. Knopf, 1998.
Sleuth Sammy and her friends trick-or-treat on Halloween and come upon a mugging and robbery by someone in a skeleton costume. With the help of her police officer friend, Sammy identifies the thief and returns the stolen goods to the owner.

Additional Titles by Wendelin Van Draanen

Sammy Keyes and the Curse of Moustache Mary. Alfred A. Knopf, 2000.
Sammy Keyes and the Runaway Elf. Alfred A. Knopf, 2000.
Sammy Keyes and the Sisters of Mercy. Alfred A. Knopf, 1999.

Teacher Resources About Relationships and Friendships

Ammon, Bette D. and Gale W. Sherman. *Worth a Thousand Words: An Annotated Guide to Picture Books for Older Readers.* Libraries Unlimited, 1996.
Canfield, Jack. *Chicken Soup for the Soul.* Health Communications, 1993.
Frankel, Fred. *Good Friends Are Hard to Find: Help Your Child Find, Make, and Keep Friends.* Perspective Publishing, 1996.

Herald, Diana Tixier. *Teen Genreflecting: A Guide to Reading Interests in Genre Fiction.* Libraries Unlimited, 1997.

Thompson, Michael. *Best Friends, Worst Enemies: Understanding the Social Lives of Children.* Ballantine Books, 2001.

Simmons, Rachel. *Odd Girl Out: The Hidden Culture of Aggression in Girls.* Harcourt Brace, 2002.

Web Sites About Relationships and Friendships

Parenting Site—Information about Children and Friendships
http://www.aboutourkids.org/articles/friends.html
Forever Friends by Lauren Short
http://www.suite101.com/topic_page.cfm/6319/3323

Web Sites About Wendelin Van Draanen

Interview with Wendelin Van Draanen at Amazon.com
http://www.amazon.com/exec/obidos/show-interview/v-w-andraanen-delin/103–0985017–1568642
Conversation with Wendelin Van Draanen
http://www.writerswrite.com/journal/dec01/vandraanen.htm
Wendelin Van Draanen
http://www.girlstart.com/wendelin.asp
Wendelin Van Draanen
http://www.girltech.com/Girl_Galaxy/GG_girls_at_work16.html
Flipped—Book Review
http://www.bookpage.com/0111bp/children/flipped.html
Meet Authors and Illustrators—Wendelin Van Draanen
http://www.childrenslit.com/f_vandraanen.html
Flipped Book and Author
http://www.randomhouse.com/teens/catalog/display.pperl?isbn=0375811745

Contact Publisher:

Knopf Books for Young Readers
Random House, Inc.
1540 Broadway
New York, NY 10036

4

A Long Way from Chicago: A Novel in Stories by Richard Peck (Dial Books for Young Readers, 1998)

Genres: Historical Fiction, Humor
Theme: The Great Depression

Introduction

This book club might coincide with the study of the Great Depression in social studies. The book *A Long Way from Chicago* gives readers an intimate view of life in the Midwest during the depression years. The content-area activities will help students understand more about this difficult time in our history. Web sites include headlines, prices, and popular songs from the Great Depression. There is a bibliography of titles, some annotated, from the time of the Great Depression. There are Web sites about Richard Peck and a bibliography of titles, some annotated, by Richard Peck.

Summary of *A Long Way from Chicago*

Every summer from 1929 to 1935, Joey Dowdel and his younger sister, Mary Alice, are sent to spend a week with their grandmother in her small Illinois town located halfway between Chicago and St. Louis. Not even the big-city crimes of Chicago offer as much excitement as Grandma Dowdel when she outwits the banker, sets illegal fish traps, catches the town's poker-playing businessmen in their underwear, and saves the town from the terror of the Cowgill boys. Now an old man, Joe Dowdel remembers those seven summers and the larger-than-life woman who outsmarted the law and used blackmail to help those in need.

Information About Richard Peck

Born in Decatur, Illinois, Richard Peck has written over eighteen novels for young readers. He is the winner of the 1990 Margaret A. Edwards Award, a prestigious award sponsored by the Young Adult Library Services Association of the American Library Association in cooperation with *School Library Journal;* the 1990 National Council of Teachers of English/ALAN Award for outstanding contributions to young adult literature; and the Mystery Writers of America Edgar Allan Poe Award.

Peck says, "I want to write novels that ask honest questions about serious issues. A novel is never an answer; it's always a question."

Discussion Questions

- Have you ever spent a summer away from home? What was it like?
- Do you know anyone who acts like Joey?
- This story is made up of several short stories about each summer Mary Alice and Joey visited Grandma. Was that a good way organize the book?
- What did you learn about life in the Great Depression years?
- Why does Sheriff Dickerson call Grandma Dowdel a one-woman crime wave?
- Do you think there actually might have been a character like Grandma, or did the author create her?
- Are there any similarities between you and Joey or Mary Alice? If so, what?
- Which character in this book taught you the most?
- Why do you think this book won the Newbery award?

Content Area Connections

Social Studies

Students may:

- Create a timeline of the years from 1929 to 1935 and list all the important national events that happened during those years.
- Research one of those events in detail and present the information to their classmates in a creative way.

Math

Students may:

- Determine the cost of the 1929 Hupmobile at that time and the average weekly salary for a worker. Would they be able to afford one? Figure out how they would do it, noting prices for necessary items for the times.

Science

Students may:

* Research the dust bowl and the five-state region it covered. Describe it and tell what happened as a result.

Language Arts

Students may:

* Create a journal with five entries telling about their life as if they lived in the early 1930s.
* Write a feature story for the Piatt County Call newspaper about Mary Alice and Royce's wedding at Grandma Dowdel's house.
* Choose a short selection from the book and read it aloud to their classmates. Select a passage that is humorous as well as descriptive of the story or a particular character.

Art

Students may:

* Design a program cover for the graduation ceremony in the 1930s, illustrating the motto of Mary Alice's high school graduating class: "We Finish—Only to Begin."
* Fold a sheet of paper into eight sections and create a comic strip of the story.

Technology

Students may:

* Research the Great Depression on the Internet. Create a chart or report to share the information with their classmates.

Mapping

Students may:

* Make a timeline of the important national events from 1929 to 1935.

Snack: Apple brown betty, apple crisp, cherry tarts

Annotated Titles About the Great Depression

Booth, David. *The Dust Bowl.* Kids Can Press Ltd., 1996.
Matthew is worried that they will have to sell the farm because of the drought. His grandfather reassures him by telling the story of what it was like during the

depression. They experienced drought, winds, extremely cold winters, and grasshoppers. Although other farmers were giving up and moving away, Grandpa wouldn't leave, and two years later the land was producing and the drought was over. "The rain will come. If not this year, then next year. We can hang on."

Brennan, Kristine. *The Stock Market Crash of 1929.* Chelsea House Publishers, 2000.

Carefully organized and clearly written, this describes the events leading up to the crash; the actual events of Black Thursday; the depression, including farm foreclosures and food lines; and then the first one hundred days of the Presidency of Franklin Delano Roosevelt. There is even a chapter titled "Could It Happen Again?" The book also includes a chronology of events and a glossary of stock market terms.

Hesse, Karen. *Out of the Dust.* Scholastic Incorporated, 1997.

This is one year in the life of 14-year-old Billy Jo. She lives on a farm in the midst of the Great Depression in the Oklahoma dust bowl. After 14 years, her Ma is pregnant. Ma copes with the dust and accepts a position in life less than she had hoped for. On a day in July, Daddy puts a pail of kerosene next to the stove. Ma, thinking it is water, begins to pour it to make coffee, but instead "Ma made a rope of fire." Ma runs outside screaming for Daddy. Billy Jo grabs the kerosene pail and throws it out the door. Unbeknownst to Billy Jo, Ma is returning to the kitchen, and the burning kerosene goes all over her. Ma is burned all down the front of her, and Billy Jo, who had a promising career as a pianist, burns her hands. Ma and the baby brother both die a month later in childbirth. There is no one to raise and comfort Billy Jo. Her father barely talks because he is so involved in his own grief and maintaining the farm during the drought. Billy Jo is so desperate to leave that she catches a freight train west. She arrives in Arizona and realizes that getting away isn't any better. She decides to return home. At last, she forgives Daddy for leaving the kerosene pail and forgives herself for all that happened later. A 1997 Newbery Award winner.

Hunt, Irene. *No Promises in the Wind.* Berkley Books, 1970.

Josh Grondowski, fifteen years old, has to make his way in the early 1930s depression years. His family is destitute because of the grinding poverty caused by the depression. He leaves to try to make it on his own and must struggle to survive in the turbulent times.

Koller, Jackie French. *Nothing to Fear.* Harcourt, 1991.

The Great Depression in New York City forces Danny Garvey's father to leave the family to look for work. Danny becomes the man of the house, helping with his younger sister and his mother's laundry business and trying to earn a few pennies by shining shoes. Danny's mother has to stop working because of pregnancy and Danny is forced to beg for food for his family. Then a stranger arrives at their door asking for help and the Garveys do not know what to do. If only Father would return to help them.

Myers, Anna. *Red-Dirt Jessie.* Walker, 1992.

Jessie, a twelve-year-old girl, tries to assist her mother with the farm in dusty Oklahoma during the Great Depression. Jessie's father suffered a nervous breakdown when Jessie's younger sister died. Jessie tries to tame an abandoned, wild dog named Ring in the hopes that the dog will help her heal her father's spirit.

Porter, Tracey. *Treasures in the Dust.* Joanna Cotler Books, 1997.

The location is rural Oklahoma and the time is the Great Depression. Annie, who is eleven, and her friend Violet tell of the dust storms and drought they endure as their families try to survive during the 1930s.

Snyder, Zilpha Keatley. *Cat Running.* Bantam Doubleday Dell Books for Young Readers, 1994.

It is during the depression, and Cat Kinsey is possibly the fastest sixth-grade runner. When she asks permission to wear slacks in the upcoming Play Day race, her father says no. Cat is furious. She goes down to the creek to get away and in the process discovers a secret grotto near the Okie camp. Okietown is made up of shacks and tents where the dust bowl refugees live. Cat lugs an old yellow playhouse to the grotto and reassembles it. On the day of the races, Cat does not run but is furious when the new Okie kid, Zane Perkins, wins the same race and title she did last year. Her anger is replaced by shock when she escapes to her grotto and finds a small ragged little Okie boy, Sammy, trying to get into her playhouse. Cat learns that Sammy is Zane's sister and pretends to be a boy because she must wear all her brother's hand-me-downs. All at once Cat's life seems to be full of Perkinses. Gradually her attitude about Okies changes, and when Sammy develops pneumonia, Zane and Cat run all the way from Okietown to call Dr. Wilson in hopes that he will help Sammy.

Stanley, Jerry. *Children of the Dust Bowl: The True Story of the School at Weedpatch Camp.* Crown Publishers, Inc., 1992.

This is the story of the migrant workers who traveled from the dust bowl in Oklahoma to California in the Great Depression. The federal government built a labor camp (Weedpatch Camp) and a school (Weedpatch School) for them. The camp housed three hundred people in one-room tin cabins or tents on wooden platforms. The school was built to keep the Okies out of the California public school system. There are many photos depicting the hard times during the depression.

Taylor, Mildred. *Let the Circle Be Unbroken.* Puffin Books, 1991.

In 1935, the Logan family watches as a friend is charged with murder and tried by an all-white jury. This story is a sequel to *Roll of Thunder, Hear My Cry.*

Wells, Rosemary. *Wingwalker.* Hyperion Books for Children, 2002.

In this short fiction book, Ruben wins a chance to ride in the passenger seat of a two-seat plane. Afterward Ruben vows he will not go higher than his attic window, if only God will keep him away from airplanes. The rest of the story tells how Ruben's family is forced to leave Ambler, Oklahoma, during the depression and how it came to be that Ruben stood on the wing of the "Land of Cotton" and for one moment was a wingwalker.

Additional Titles About the Great Depression

Andryszewski, Tricia. *The Dust Bowl: Disaster on the Plains.* Millbrook Press Inc., 1993.

Appelt, Kathi A. *Down Cut Shin Creek: Pack Horse Librarians of Kentucky.* HarperCollins Children's Book Group, 2001.

Blackwood, Gary L. *Moonshine.* Cavendish Children's Books, 1999.

Cochrane, Pat A. *Purely Rosie Pearl.* Bantam Doubleday Dell Books for Young Readers, 1996.

Collins, Pat. *Just Imagine.* Houghton Mifflin Company, 2001.

DeFelice, Cynthia. *Nowhere to Call Home.* HarperCollins Children's Book Group, 2001.

De Young, C. Coco. *A Letter to Mrs. Roosevelt.* Bantam Doubleday Dell Books for Young Readers, 2001.

Duey, Kathleen. *Agnes May Gleason: Walsenburg, Colorado, 1933.* Turtleback Books, 1998.

Durbin, William. *The Journal of C. J. Jackson: A Dust Bowl Migrant, Oklahoma to California, 1935.* Scholastic Incorporated, 2002.

Lyon, George Ella. *Borrowed Children.* Orchard Books, 1988.

Meltzer, Milton. *Brother Can You Spare a Dime: The Great Depression of 1929-1933.* Facts on File, 1990.

Moss, Marissa. *Rose's Journal: The Story of a Girl in the Great Depression.* Harcourt Children's Books, 2001.

Recorvits, Barbara. *Goodbye, Walter Malinsk.* Farrar Straus Giroux, 1999.

Sonnenfeld, Kelly. *Memories of Clason Point.* Penguin Putnam Books for Young Readers, 1998.

Taylor, Kim. *Cissy Funk.* HarperCollins Children's Book Group, 2001.

Taylor, Mildred. *Roll of Thunder, Hear My Cry.* Dial Books for Young Readers, 1996.

Thesman, Jean. *The Storyteller's Daughter.* Houghton Mifflin Company, 1997.

Thrasher, Crystal. *End of a Dark Road.* Margaret K. McElderry, 1982.

Turnbull, Ann. *Speedwell.* Candlewick Press, 1992.

Westall, Robert. *Christmas Spirit: Two Stories.* Farrar Straus Giroux, 1994.

Willis, Patricia. *The Barn Burner.* Houghton Mifflin Company, 2000.

Wormser, Richard L. *Growing Up in the Great Depression.* Atheneum Books for Young Readers, 1994.

Annotated Titles by Richard Peck

A Year Down Yonder. Dial Books for Young Readers, 2000.

The year is 1937 and Mary Alice has come to stay with Grandma by herself because Joey has gone to work with the Civilian Conservation Corps. Mary Alice brings her radio and her cat and knows life with Grandma will not be easy. She attends the town's school and is referred to as the rich girl from Chicago. She ends up helping Grandma with her plans to run the town her own way and sees that Grandma really has a heart of gold.

Are You in the House Alone? Puffin Books, 2000.

A high school girl named Gail receives threatening notes and phone calls and realizes she is constantly being watched. Even though she is surrounded by friends and family, she finds herself totally alone.

The Dreadful Future of Blossom Culp. Puffin Books, 2001.

Teenage psychic Blossom Culp is visiting a deserted mansion on Halloween in the year 1914 with her friend Alexander. Suddenly she is sucked into a time warp that takes her into the future—today—and she has to use her psychic powers to try to get back to her friend.

Fair Weather. Dial Books for Young Readers, 2001.

Thirteen-year-old Rosie Beckett and her family take a trip from the farm to the big city in 1893 to see the Chicago World's Fair. Rosie comes face to face with some of the well-known characters of the time and sees many breathtaking and bewildering sights.

Father Figure. Puffin Books, 1996.

Seventeen-year-old Jim Atwater has looked after his brother Byron since he was born. Their dad had left but returned when their mother died. Their grandmother has made plans for the summer, so Jim and Byron go to stay with their father in Miami for the summer. This is the story of their getting to know their dad while they explore the Coconut Grove area of Miami.

The Ghost Belonged to Me. Puffin Books, 1996.

In this first story in the Blossom Culp series, Alexander sees an eerie glow from the window of the barn and goes to investigate. He finds a female ghost who tells him of great danger that lies ahead. Will Alexander be able to save himself?

Ghosts I Have Been. Puffin Books, 2001.

Another story about Blossom Culp, who has learned she has the gift of sight: she can see the unseen. But she also learns that although she can see what is going to happen, she is powerless to change the course of history. In this story she is there when the Titanic sinks.

The Great Interactive Dream Machine: Another Adventure in Cyberspace. Puffin Books, 1998.

This is a sequel to *Lost in Cyberspace.* Computer whiz Aaron Zimmer accidentally gives his computer the power to grant wishes. Aaron and his friend Josh discover that the computer has a few bugs and that they are being watched by a puzzling spy.

Teacher Resource About the Great Depression

Adamson, Lynda. *Literature Connections to World History Grades 7–12.* Libraries Unlimited, 1998.

Web Sites About the Great Depression

Links to Great Depression Resources
http://www.sos.state.mi.us/history/museum/techstuf/depressn/gd_links.
html
The Great Depression News
http://www.sos.state.mi.us/history/museum/explore/museums/
hismus/1900–75/depressn/labnews2.html
Songs of the Great Depression
http://www.library.csi.cuny.edu/dept/history/lavender/cherries.html
America's Great Depression Timeline
http://www.amatecon.com/GD/gdtimeline.html
Surviving the Dust Bowl
http://www.pbs.org/wgbh/amex/dustbowl/
Savannah Morning News Headlines of the 1930s
http://www.savannahnow.com/features/150years/1930depress.shtml
Headlines—Stock Market Crash—1929
http://bss.sfsu.edu/tygiel/Hist427/texts/crashheadlines.htm
Brother, Can You Spare a Dime? Recorded by Bing Crosby
http://bss.sfsu.edu/tygiel/Hist427/427sound/Crashsound/brother.html

Web Sites About Richard Peck

Authors/Illustrators—Richard Peck
http://www.randomhouse.com/teachers/authors/peck.html
Featured Author: Richard Peck
http://www.carolhurst.com/authors/rpeck.html
Margaret A. Edwards Award: Richard Peck
http://www.carr.lib.md.us/mae/peck/peck.htm
Richard Peck: Newbery Award Winning Author
http://www.richardpeck.smartwriters.com/
Reading Guides—A Long Way from Chicago and A Year Down Yonder
http://www.penguinputnam.com/Author/AuthorFrame?0000020017

Contact Publisher:

Penguin Putnam Books for Young Readers
375 Hudson Street
New York, NY 10014

5

Among the Hidden by Margaret Peterson Haddix (Simon & Schuster Juvenile, 1998)

Genre: Science Fiction
Theme: The Future

Introduction

Science fiction has always been a popular genre, possibly because it can include so many different types of storylines. Usually the story takes place at an undetermined time in the future after some sort of major change. *Among the Hidden* takes a look at the future with an emphasis on population control as the world population escalates. Haddix has four books in this Shadow Children series with the same theme. The listed titles, some annotated, provide many excellent stories about events in the future. Haddix also has written other books with a futuristic theme.

Summary of *Among the Hidden*

In a society that allows only two children per family, Luke is a third child, a "shadow child." He's illegal, strictly forbidden. So he stays hidden, alone most of the time and frightened all the time. Then one day he discovers another shadow child, Jen, living in one of the fancy new houses the government built behind his family's farm. Luke and Jen quickly become friends, but Jen is bold and daring and wants more than companionship from Luke. She wants him to be a crusader, another third child willing to risk everything for freedom.

Information About Margaret Peterson Haddix

Margaret Haddix grew up on a farm outside Washington Courthouse. She graduated from Miami University (of Ohio) in 1986 with degrees in English/Creative Writing, English/Journalism, and History. After college she worked as a journalist, first as a copy editor for the Fort Wayne (Indiana) *Journal Gazette* and then as a reporter for *The Indianapolis News*. When Margaret and her husband moved to Illinois in 1991, she began focusing more on writing fiction while she was doing freelance business writing and working part-time as a community college instructor. She and her family later moved to Scranton, Pennsylvania, before returning to Ohio in 1998.

Her husband, Doug, is now a special projects editor at a newspaper, *The Columbus Dispatch*. They have two children, Meredith and Conor.

Discussion Questions

- Where and when do you think this story takes place?
- Why is Luke's family afraid of the government?
- What kind of relationship does Luke have with his family?
- Would you have joined Jen in her march on the president's house?
- What do you think of Jen's stepfather if he is a member of the Population Police and also the father of a third child?
- What questions do you still have about this story?
- How would you describe the mood of this story?
- Do you think the author has a message? If so, what is it?
- What choices did Luke really have?
- What do you think of Luke's parents?
- What will happen to Luke after the book ends?

Content Area Connections

Language Arts

Students may:

- Write a short story telling what they think the next book will be about. (This is the first in a series of books called *The Shadow Children: Among the Hidden, Among the Imposters, Among the Betrayed, and Among the Barons.*)
- Write a story about what they think the world will be like in the future.
- Create a story-related crossword puzzle or word search to share with their classmates.

Social Studies

Students may:

- Do some research and find out why China has a law that strictly limits family size. After they have found the reason, do they agree or disagree with this policy?
- Research totalitarianism—the type of government that exists at the time of the story—and compare and contrast totalitarianism and democracy. Could the United States implement a population law and employ population police in the future?

Art

Students may:

- Create a government-sponsored poster, bumper sticker, or billboard warning people about the third child.
- Create an ad for the book that would be featured in a science fiction magazine.

Technology

Students may:

- Research the world population on the Internet. Prepare a presentation about what is happening and the effect of an increasing population on natural resources and the environment.

Mapping

Students may:

- Create a concept map of the future, perhaps 100 years from now. Make the second layer homes, school, technology, food, and so on, and brainstorm to come up with all the changes they think might take place.

    Snack: Potato chips

Annotated Titles About the Future

Cart, Michael. *Tomorrowland: Ten Stories About the Future.* Scholastic Press, 1999.

Michael Cart, author and former director of the Beverly Hills Public Library, has compiled these short stories from famous young adult authors such as Jon Sciesszka, Rodman Philbrick, Lois Lowry, Tor Seidler, Gloria Skurzynski, Ron Koertge, Katherine Paterson, Jacqueline Woodson, and James Cross Giblin. The stories vary in their approach to tomorrowland. Several of the authors look to the past and see what the ancients imagined the future to be. Some of the authors select the present day, and others reach out to a time in the past. One particularly disturbing story is "The Last Book in the Universe" by Rodman Philbrick. His story answers the questions "What if there came a time when no one read books? What if books and the whole concept of reading had been forgotten? What would the world be like? What would the people be like?" At the end of each story, the authors tell what prompted them to write the story in the Author's Note. At the conclusion of many of the stories, you do not want them to end and maybe they are actually the beginning.

Farmer, Nancy. *The Ear, the Eye, and the Arm.* Crestwood House, 1992.

This story takes place in Zimbabwe in the year 2195. Siblings Tendai, Rita, and Kuda, children of General Amadeus Matsika, the country's Chief of Security, embark on an adventure. (African Shona mythology inspired the story. The Shona were the most powerful political group—80 percent of the population—when Zimbabwe became independent in 1980.) When the three overprotected siblings start out on their first excursion by themselves, they are kidnapped by the She-elephant who rules the once-toxic waste dump where plastic was mined. The mother and father hire a detective agency—the Ear, the Eye, and the Arm—whose agents are always one step behind the children. This is a long and unusual story.

Levitan, Sonia. *The Cure.* Silver Whistle, 1999.

It is the year 2407, and Gemm 16884 has just experienced that dream again. Even when he was young, Gemm knew he was different because he loved music, rhythms, and singing. Because diversity is evil in the eyes of the elders, Gemm is offered a chance to redeem himself by partaking in the Cure. Gemm agrees, and he returns to an age when music and love offset the evil and squalor. Gemm becomes Johannes, a Jew living in Strasbourg, Germany. It is the time of the black plague, 1348. As the plague spreads throughout Europe, the Jews are blamed for it, and terror and evil reign. Johannes and his community suffer and die, and Gemm returns to the futuristic society, supposedly cured. Gemm knows that "diversity can lead to emotions and emotions can bring us either to hatred or love. People must have that choice." Will it begin all over again for Gemm?

Lowry, Lois. *The Giver.* Houghton Mifflin Company, 1993.

Twelve-year-old Jonas lives in a seemingly ideal world. Not until he is given his life assignment as the Receiver does he begin to understand the dark secrets behind this fragile community.

Naylor, Phyllis Reynolds. *Sang Spell.* Atheneum Books for Young Readers, 1998.

Josh's mother is killed in an auto accident, so Josh hitchhikes to Texas to begin a new life. He is mugged and left for dead along a road deep in Appalachia. He awakens in a primitive village inhabited by the persecuted Melungeons. The people seem to be under a spell as they maintain the old ways of planting and harvesting wild ginseng. Josh soon feels that these people are no longer his rescuers but his captors.

Nicholson, William. *The Wind Singer.* Hyperion Books for Children, 2000.

All the people strove hard and reached higher for the glory of Aramanth except the Hath family. When Kestrel Hath forgets her homework, Dr. Batch, the teacher, makes an example of her. He reorders the seating in class based on points and how hard the students try. On her own, Kestrel rebels and moves to the bottom of the class beside Mumpo, the outcast and friendless. Dr. Batch continues to attack Kestrel until she leaves school in anger with Mumpo and Bowman, her brother. Kestrel goes to the center of town, climbs the famous wind-singer structure, and out of frustration yells rude words through the horns, which carry the sound throughout the city. Kestrel must be punished and broken for the good of all. Thus begins the journey of Kestrel, Mumpo, and Bowman to find the silver voice of the Wind Singer to bring about change and restore the old ways of Aramanth.

Nix, Garth. *Shade's Children.* HarperCollins Children's Book Group, 1997.

This is a dark story of a post-nuclear war world ruled by Overlords who take children's brains and bodies to create monsters who fight for their masters. Shade is not really human but a holographic image coming from a computer. Shade provides food and shelter in an abandoned submarine for children who try to get information about the Overlords. Finally, the children set out to try on their own to destroy the Overlords.

Shusterman, Neal. *Downsiders: A Novel.* Simon & Schuster Books for Young Readers, 1999.

Beneath New York City lies a strange and secret world called Downside. The people who live there know it is forbidden to go Topside, but 14-year-old Talon is curious about what goes on above ground. He searches for medicine for his sister Pidge, who has flu-like symptoms. Lindsay, also 14, has just been dumped in New York City by her newly divorced, career-student mother to live with her father and stepbrother. She makes friends with Talon and supplies him with some left-over antibiotics, and eventually he takes her for a forbidden visit to Downside. Lindsay's dad is a city engineer working on an underground aqueduct. During his excavating he discovers Downside, and the future of Downside and its inhabitants is in question.

Sleator, William. *The Beasties.* Dutton Children's Books, 1997.

Doug and Colette have been warned about the Beasties who live in the woods behind old houses. Soon after their family moves to the woods, Colette becomes involved with the Beasties, or "family" as they like to be called. Doug tries to protect Colette because the Beasties require human body parts to survive. He goes on a mission to collect information about the logging camp that is responsible for the Beasties' health problems. The Beasties' horror is real, and Doug is ready to sacrifice his eye to help perpetuate the colony of Beasties.

Smith, Roland. *Sasquatch.* Hyperion, 1998.

Thirteen-year-old Dylan follows his father into the woods on the slopes of Mount St. Helens, which is on the brink of another eruption, in an attempt to protect the resident Sasquatch from ruthless hunters.

Stevermer, Caroline. *River Rats.* Harcourt Brace and Company, 1992.

The River Rats are orphans who run a coal-driven paddle wheeler up and down the toxic Mississippi River after the Flash, a nuclear holocaust. Without incident, they deliver music and occasionally mail to the safe communities until the day they rescue King from the river and encounter the "Lesters" who were following him.

Additional Titles About the Future

Bawden, Nina. *Off the Road.* Clarion Books, 1998.
Bell, Hilari. *A Matter of Profit.* HarperCollins Children's Book Group, 2001.
Billingsley, Franny. *Well Wished.* Thorndike Press, 2001.
Bradbury, Ray. *The Martian Chronicles.* Doubleday, 1950.
Brittain, Bill. *Shape-changer.* HarperCollins Publishers, 1994.
Butler, Susan. *The Hermit Thrush Sings.* Bantam Doubleday Books for Young Readers, 2001.
Butts, Nancy. *The Door in the Lake.* Penguin Putnam Books for Young Readers, 2000.
Card, Orson Scott. *Ender's Game.* Tor Books, 1985.
Christopher, John. *The White Mountains.* Macmillan Publishing Company, 1967.
Coville, Bruce. *Bruce Coville's UFOs.* Morrow Avon, 2000.
Dexter, Catherine. *Alien Game.* Morrow Junior Books, 1995.
Dickinson, Peter. *Eva.* Delacorte Press, 1989.
Gutman, Dan. *Virtually Perfect.* Hyperion Books for Children, 1998.
Hughes, Monica. *The Golden Aquarians.* Simon & Schuster Books for Young Readers, 1995.

———. *Invitation to the Game.* Simon & Schuster Books for Young Readers, 1991.

Ibbotson, Iva. *The Secret of Platform 13.* Thorndike Press, 2001.

Jones, Diana Wynne. *Hexwood.* Greenwillow Books, 1994.

———. *A Tale of Time City.* HarperCollins Children's Book Group, 2002.

Kerner, Charlotte. *Blueprint.* Lerner Publishing Group, 2000.

Klause, Annette Curtis. *Alien Secrets.* Delacorte Press, 1993.

Lasky, Kathryn. *Star Split.* Hyperion Books for Children, 2001.

Lawrence, Louise. *Dream-Weaver.* Clarion Books, 1996.

Mahy, Margaret. *Aliens in the Family.* Scholastic Incorporated, 1986.

———. *The Greatest Show Off Earth.* Viking Press, 1994.

McCaffrey, Anne. *Pegasus in Flight.* Ballantine Books, 1990.

Miller, Ron. *The History of Science Fiction.* Franklin Watts, 2001.

Paulsen, Gary. *Transall Saga.* Delacorte Press, 1998.

———. *The White Fox Chronicles.* Random House Books for Young Readers, 2002.

Read into the Millennium: Tales of the Future. Millbrook Press Inc., 1999.

Shusterman, Neal. *The Dark Side of Nowhere: A Novel.* Little, Brown, 1997.

Skurzynski, Gloria. *The Virtual War.* Simon & Schuster Books for Young Readers, 1997.

Sleator, William. *Singularity.* Dutton Children's Books, 1985.

———. *The Boxes.* Dutton Children's Books, 1998.

———. *Marco's Millions.* Penguin Putnam Books for Young Readers, 2001.

Thompson, Colin. *Future Eden: A Brief History of Next Time.* Simon & Schuster Books for Young Readers, 2000.

Westwood, Chris. *Virtual World.* Viking Press, 1997.

Williams, Mark L. *Ancient Fire: Danger Boy, No. 1.* Tricycle Books, 2001.

Annotated Titles by Margaret Peterson Haddix

Among the Betrayed. Simon & Schuster Books for Young Readers, 2002.
Thirteen-year-old Nina is being held prisoner by the Population Police and she is given a choice: help them identify other shadow children or die. She is put in a cold, damp basement cell with three younger children whom she must betray. Instead they escape and run, and Nina finds that the younger children are extremely resourceful and knowledgeable as they try to find safety.

Among the Imposters. Simon & Schuster Books for Young Readers, 2001.
Luke has taken the identity of a boy who was killed in a skiing accident, and Jen's father helps him get into a school for boys. He tries to fit in but the other boys are strange and rude and take great pleasure in belittling him. Eventually he finds a group of boys who are third children, and they are impressed that Luke knew Jen. The boys claim they are working on ways to defy the Population Police, and Luke is comforted by this idea. But soon he learns something disturbing about one of the boys and he has to act quickly and decisively.

Don't You Dare Read This, Mrs. Dunphrey. Simon & Schuster Juvenile, 1996.
English teacher Mrs. Dunphrey requires each student to keep a journal, prom-

ising that she will not read entries that the students mark Do Not Read. Tish Bonner, an underachieving student, discovers that journal writing is a great way to relieve the pressures in her life. She fills the pages with details of her troubled life with her severely depressed mother and abusive father. She eventually decides to seek help for herself and her brother by letting her teacher read her journal.

Just Ella. Simon & Schuster Juvenile, 1999.

In this retelling of Cinderella, fifteen-year-old Ella discovers that life with Prince Charming is not at all as she expected. She is bored with embroidery and palace protocol and finds the prince to be dull. She falls in love with her tutor, Jed Reston, takes charge of her life, and walks away from her politically arranged marriage to fulfill her dreams with Jed.

Leaving Fishers. Aladdin Paperbacks, 1997.

Dorry moved from Ohio and is new at Crestwood High. She is having a hard time adjusting until a group called the Fishers begins to invite her to sit and eat with them at school. Gradually she is doing more and more with the group and attending their church and Bible study classes and submitting to the strict demands of her discipler, Angela. In spite of her doubts, Dorry continues to adhere to the Fishers and donates her college fund to the church. Under pressure to convert someone, she begins to tell the children she is babysitting for about God and the fires of Hell. This is a turning point for Dorry and she realizes the harm she is doing to herself and family. Slowly Dorry realizes she has been involved in a cult and was brainwashed into believing and doing what the Fishers wanted her to.

Running Out of Time. Simon & Schuster Juvenile, 1995.

Jessie grows up in a reconstructed village from 1840 that serves as a tourist attraction. Jessie believes it is really 1840. The families in the village are not allowed to leave. When a medical emergency occurs, Jessie's mom sends her out of the village for help. Jessie learns it is 1996 and the village inhabitants are part of a scientific experiment.

Takeoffs and Landings. Simon & Schuster Juvenile, 2001.

Chuck and Lori, who live on their grandparents' farm, go on their first plane trip to join their mother, who is a motivational speaker. She is on a two-week, five-city trip. Chuck and Lori's father died eight years ago and they are upset that their mother's career keeps her away from home most of the time. During their time together they finally face some issues regarding their father.

Turnabout. Simon & Schuster Juvenile, 2000.

In the year 2000, a group of nursing home residents are given an experimental injection as part of Project Turnabout. The injection reverses aging. Melly and Anny Beth, aged 100 and 103 at the time of the injection, are now teenagers in the year 2085. Everyone who has received the injection dies, so Melly and Anny Beth must prepare for their inevitable return to infancy.

Additional Titles by Margaret Peterson Haddix

Among the Barons. Simon & Schuster Books for Young Readers, 2003.
Because of Anya. Simon & Schuster Juvenile, 2002.

Teacher Resource About the Future

Murray, Janet. *Hamlet on the Holodeck: The Future of Narrative in Cyberspace.* MIT Press, 2000.

Web Sites About the Future

Visions of the Future
http://www.cbc4kids.cbc.ca/general/time/millennium/predictions.html
Beyond 2000
http://www.nationalgeographic.com/world/9901/beyond-2000/beyond-2000-icons.html
China's One Child Policy
http://www.overpopulation.com/faq/population_control/one_child.html

Web Sites About Margaret Peterson Haddix

Margaret Peterson Haddix's Summer Reading List
http://www.kidsreads.com/features/010620-haddix-margaret.asp
Margaret Peterson Haddix
http://library.thinkquest.org/J0110073/Author.html
Margaret Peterson Haddix
http://www.simonsays.com/subs/author.cfm?areaid = 183&isbn = 0689839049

Contact Publisher:

Simon & Shuster Books for Young Readers
1230 Avenue of the Americas
New York, NY 10020
http://www.SimonSaysKids.com

6

A Time Apart by Diane Stanley
(Morrow Junior Books, 1999)

Genre: Family
Theme: Archaeology

Introduction

This book club might coincide with a social studies unit on archaeology or the Iron Age. Other stories have been written about reenactments of life in various periods in history. After reading this book, students might want to speculate on what life was like and how difficult it would be to pretend to live in days of long ago—even for a real science experiment.

There are many possible related activities, including a visit to a re-created village or even an archaeological dig in your area. If that is not possible, there are videos about life in different eras of history. There are great Web sites and videos provided by public television on the Iron Age and this particular experiment.

Summary of *A Time Apart*

Ginny's mother is undergoing treatments for cancer, so she sends Ginny to England to live with her dad, who is a professor living in a year-long experimental Iron Age village. Thirteen-year-old Ginny is upset about leaving her friends in Houston, Texas, to live with strangers and her dad—whom she hasn't seen in a year—in this strange setting. Yet she actually finds herself enjoying it; she is a good cook and makes friends with a younger child, an older teenager, and adult members of the group. When she runs away to go home to her mother, her dad comes after her and goes too. She realizes her mother needs time to work through her treatments, so Ginny returns with her father to England and finishes out the time. All through the story you get a clear picture of what life is thought to have been like in an Iron Age village.

Information About Diane Stanley

Diane Stanley is the author and illustrator of more than forty books for children, noted especially for her series of picture-book biographies. *Shaka, King of the Zulus* was named a *New York Times* Best Illustrated Book, and *Leonardo da Vinci* received the Orbis Pictus Award for Outstanding Nonfiction for Children from the National Council of Teachers of English. Ten of her books have been honored as Notable Books by the American Library Association, and she has twice received both the Boston Globe-Horn Book Award and the Society of Children's Book Writers and Illustrators' Golden Kite Award. She was the recipient of the Washington Post-Children's Book Guild Award for Nonfiction for the body of her work. A selection of her paintings was recently exhibited at the National Center for Children's Illustrated Literature and is currently on tour. Her art was featured in an exhibit at the National Museum of Women in the Arts in Washington, D.C.

Diane was born in Abilene, Texas. She earned her bachelor's degree from Trinity University and her M.A. in Medical and Biological Illustration from Johns Hopkins University College of Medicine. She has worked as a medical illustrator, a graphic designer for Dell Publishing, and an art director at G.P. Putnam's Sons, winning three design awards from the New York Book Show.

She lives in Houston, Texas, with her husband, Peter Vennema, who sometimes collaborates with her on the research for her biographies. She has three grown children, Catherine, Tamara, and John.

Discussion Questions

- What were some factors that made it difficult for Ginny to go to England?
- Do you think the title is appropriate for this story?
- How does the story setting change?
- Describe the main character.
- What did you learn about life in the Iron Age from this story?
- What choices did Ginny have in the story?
- What was the most important part of the story?
- What lessons does this story teach about life?
- Were there twists and turns in the story that surprised you?
- What would you have done if you were inside the book and you could have helped Ginny?

Content Area Connections

Language Arts

Students may:

- Keep a journal of what it would have been like to live in the Iron Age; include diagrams and illustrations.
- Create a profile of a story character.

Social Studies

Students may:

- Do some research on the Iron Age. When was it? Write a description of the Iron Age.

Art

Students may:

- Draw and label a diagram of an Iron Age roundhouse.

Science

Students may:

- Make a list of crops people grew during the Iron Age in ancient England. Include the animals they had as well.
- Research archaeological digs. Find out how a dig is accomplished. Look at some famous digs and the discoveries associated with them.

Technology

Students may:

- Research the Iron Age on the Internet and create a presentation about life in those times.
- Find something about undersea archaeology: Are there any digs taking place now?

Mapping

Students may:

- Create a web of information about the Iron Age—list information about homes, food, lifestyle, social patterns, and so on.

> Snack: Dirt cake (chocolate pudding, crumbled chocolate cookies, gummy worms—served in a clay flower pot with a plastic shovel)

Annotated Titles About Archaeology

Abelove, Joan. *Go and Come Back.* DK Publishing, Inc., 1998.

The author lived in the Amazon jungle for two years. This fictional story is about two young anthropologists who ask to live in the village of Poincushmana for one year. Alicia is a young female in the tribe who adopts an unwanted baby and tells of life in the tribe. The anthropologists, who come to study the ways of the people, learn from them as well. "In the end, at the end of it all, the love you have, the friendship you have, the love you are left with, is just the same, is only the same, as the love you gave, the love, the friendship you had for others."

Batten, Mary. *Anthropologist: Scientist of the People.* Houghton Mifflin Company, 2001.

An anthropologist, Magdalena Hurtado, studies the Ache, hunter-gatherers living in Paraguay, South America. She has lived among them for fifteen years, learning the language, studying their culture and traditions, and recording their history.

Denzel, Justin. *Boy of the Painted Cave.* Philomel Books, 1988.

Tao knows he is different from the other members of the Clan. He was born with a bad foot, and his mother died in her efforts to save him. Tao knows that drawing images and using a wolf to hunt in the Slough are all taboo. If Tao is caught, he will have to face Saxon, the sacred bull, armed only with his spear. The old Shaman Graybeard meets Tao and, in spite of the taboo, teaches him to draw and paint images in the secret cave. Graybeard has chosen Tao to become the new Cave Painter but dies before he tells the Clan of his decision. Tao must face Saxon, and no one has ever defeated the mighty bull.

Dickinson, Peter. *The Kin: Suth's Story.* Grosset & Dunlap, 1998.

The Moonhawks were attacked, and many of the men were killed and the women taken away. The remaining Kin and orphaned children are on the move. Noli convinces Suth to return to the lair where the younger orphaned children were left. Now it is Suth's responsibility to forage for food and keep the five orphans safe. This is the first of four stories about the Kin. It is fascinating reading about how life might have been 200,000 years ago.

Jackson, Donna M. *The Bone Detectives: How Forensic Anthropologists Solve Crimes and Uncover Mysteries of the Dead.* Little, Brown, 1996.

Forensic anthropologists are bone detectives, able to determine a person's sex, race, age, height, weight, and cause of death from the bones. Follow the procedures of Dr. Michael Charney in an actual investigation.

Lauber, Patricia. *Painters of the Caves.* National Geographic Society, 1998.

In 1994 three friends went exploring the limestone hills near Avignon, France. This led to the discovery of what was later called Chauvet Cave after one of the explorers. They discovered more than 300 paintings of animals that lived more than 32,000 years ago. The story of the people who created these Stone Age wall paintings was pieced together through the fossils and the stone tools left behind.

Martell, Hazel Mary. *The Kingfisher Book of the Ancient World from the Ice Age to the Fall of Rome.* Kingfisher, 1995.

Includes a basic introduction to archaeology, how history is pieced together, and a section on prehistory.

Sattler, Helen Roney. *The Earliest Americans.* Clarion Books, 1993.

Did you ever wonder who the earliest Americans were, where they came from, and when they arrived? This book goes over the evidence of the most widely accepted theories.

Additional Titles About Archaeology

De Carvalho, Roberto. *Prehistory.* McGraw-Hill Children's Publishing, 2000.

Deem, James M. *Bodies from the Bog.* Houghton Mifflin Company, 1998.

Dig This!: How Archaeologists Uncover Our Past. Lerner Publishing Group, 1993.

Early Humans. Alfred A. Knopf, 1989.

Getz, David. *Frozen Man.* Henry Holt and Company, 1994.

Greenberg, Lorna and Margot F. Horwitz. *Digging into the Past: Pioneers of Archaeology.* Franklin Watts, 2001.

Hill, Pamela. *The Last Grail Keeper.* Holiday House, 2001.

Hoobler, Dorothy and Tom. *The Fact or Fiction Files: Lost Civilizations.* Walker, 1992.

Jespersen, James. *Mummies, Dinosaurs, Moon Rocks; How We Know How Old Things Are.* Atheneum Books for Young Readers, 1996.

Leroi-Gourhan, Andre. *The Hunters of Prehistory.* Atheneum Books for Young Readers, 1989.

Lessem, Don. *The Iceman.* Crown Publishing Group, Incorporated, 1994.

MacDonald, Fiona. *The Stone Age News.* Candlewick Press, 1998.

McGowen, Tom. *Adventures in Archaeology.* Twenty-First Century Books, 1997.

———. *Giant Stones and Earth Mounds.* Millbrook Press Inc, 2000.

McIntosh, Jane. *Archeology.* Alfred A. Knopf, 1994.

Patent, Dorothy Hinshaw. *Secrets of the Ice Man.* Benchmark Books, 1999.

Reinhard, Johan. *Discovering the Inca Ice Maiden: My Adventures on Ampato.* National Geographic Society, 1998.

Scheller, William G. *Amazing Archaeologists and Their Finds.* Oliver Press, 1994.

Smith, KC. *Exploring for Shipwrecks.* Franklin Watts, 2000.

Stefoff, Rebecca. *Finding the Lost Cities.* Oxford University Press, 1997.

Tanaka, Shelley. *Discovering the Iceman; What Was It Like to Find a 5,300-Year-Old Mummy?* Hyperion Books for Children, 1996.

Wilcox, Charlotte. *Mummies, Bones, and Body Parts.* Lerner Publishing Group, 2000.

Annotated Titles by Diane Stanley

Bard of Avon: The Story of William Shakespeare. Morrow Junior Books, 1992.
Diane Stanley has approached this book as a historian. Because little is known about William Shakespeare, Diane has gathered all the known facts until a pattern appears. This book follows the journey of William when he was five, marriage to Anne Hathaway at eighteen, the Globe Theatre in London, and retirement in Stratford.

Charles Dickens: The Man Who Had Great Expectations. William Morrow & Company, 1993.
This is the story of the life of Charles Dickens from his life as a twelve-year-old working in a blacking factory because his father was in debtors' prison, through his long and well-known career as a writer.

Cleopatra. William Morrow & Company, 1994.
The story begins when Cleopatra is eighteen years old and becomes the Queen of Egypt. She loses her power, raises an army with the help of Julius Caesar and Mark Antony, and attempts to return to the throne and bring Egypt back to glory until her death at age 39.

Joan of Arc. Morrow Junior Books, 1998.
After a brief background of the Hundred Year War between France and England, Stanley tells of the visions of Joan and how she was to rescue the city of

Orleans, "gateway to loyal France [which] was surrounded by the English." Joan went on to have many victories before she was turned over to the English, her enemy, and tried by the Inquisition.

The Last Princess: The Story of Princess Ka'iulani of Hawaii. Four Winds Press, 1991.

Princess Ka'iulani was the only child of Princess Miriam Lifelike, and it appeared she was to be the Queen of Hawaii. However, when her mother was dying, she foretold that Ka'iulani would go far away and be gone a long time, she would not marry, and she would not rule Hawaii.

Michelangelo. HarperCollins Publishers, 2000.

Michelangelo lived during the Renaissance and mastered painting, sculpture, and architecture.

Peter the Great. Morrow Junior Books, 1999.

Ten-year-old Peter Alexeevich was crowned czar of Russia. He traveled west to Europe, disguised as a common soldier, to learn their ways in the hope of guiding his country through social reform to greatness. He became a respected leader and built the city of St. Petersburg.

Shaka: King of the Zulus. William Morrow & Company, 1989.

Shaka was a young boy when he and his mother were banished from the Zulu tribe in the hills of southern Africa. Shaka dreamed of becoming a great warrior and became a military genius. He built the Zulu tribe into a strong nation and became a respected king of his people in the 18th century.

The True Adventure of Daniel Hall. Dial Books for Young Readers, 1995.

Daniel left home when he was fourteen and signed on for three years aboard the whaling ship the Condor. The captain was particularly harsh on Daniel, so when the opportunity arose to leave in the middle of a Siberian night, he took it. Daniel would later write, "We were free—free from a life of slavery—free from tyranny—free from the oppressive power of our fellow men." It would be years and many adventures before Daniel would make his way back to New Bedford and his friends and family.

Additional Titles by Diane Stanley

Being Thankful at Plymouth Plantation. HarperCollins Children's Book Group, 2003.

Elena. Hyperion Books for Children, 1996.

Joining the Boston Tea Party. HarperCollins Children's Book Group, 2001.

Leonardo da Vinci. HarperCollins Children's Book Group, 2000.

The Mysterious Matter of I.M. Fine. HarperCollins Children's Book Group, 2002.

Petrosinella: A Neapolitan Rapunzel. Penguin Putnam Books for Young Readers, 1995.

Roughing It on the Oregon Trail. HarperCollins Children's Book Group, 2001.

Teacher Resources About Archaeology

Breyer, Michelle. *Early Humans: Interdisciplinary Thematic Unit.* Teacher Created Materials, 1995.

Coan, Julie. *Digging into Archaeology: Hands-On, Minds-On Unit Study.* Critical Thinking Books and Software, 1999.

Web Sites About Archaeology

Surviving the Iron Age
http://www.bbc.co.uk/history/programmes/surviving_ironage/
Iron Age in Britain
http://www.bbc.co.uk/history/bytime/britain/o_iron_age.shtml

Web Sites About Diane Stanley

Diane Stanley—Books for Children
http://www.dianestanley.com/
Diane Stanley
http://www.harperchildrens.com/hch/author/author/stanley/

Contact Publisher:

HarperCollins Children's Books
1350 Avenue of the Americas
New York, NY 10019

7

Pharaoh's Daughter: A Novel of Ancient Egypt by Julius Lester (Silver Whistle, 2000)

Genre: Historical Fiction
Theme: Ancient Egypt

Introduction

Julius Lester provides a new twist to the story of Moses in *Pharaoh's Daughter.* The Ancient Egypt setting offers many activities for this book club, including informative and fun Web sites, many titles about life in Ancient Egypt, and curriculum connections from hieroglyphs to mummies. There is ample opportunity to take a closer look at Julius Lester, an author with a long list of varied titles to his credit.

Summary of *Pharaoh's Daughter*

Born into slavery, adopted as an infant by a princess, and raised in the palace of mighty Pharaoh, Moses struggles to define himself. And so do the three women who love him: his own embittered mother, forced to give him up by Pharaoh's decree; the Egyptian princess who defies her father and raises Moses as her own child; and his headstrong sister, Almah, who discovers a greater kinship with the Egyptian deities than with her own God of the Hebrews. Told by Moses and his sister Almah from alternating points of view, this stunning novel by Newbery Honor author Julius Lester probes questions of identity, faith, and destiny.

Information About Julius Lester

Julius Lester has written more than twenty books for young readers. He teaches in the English, Judaic Studies, and History departments at the University of Massachusetts in Amherst, Massachusetts. Lester was born in 1939 in St. Louis, Missouri. Growing up, he wanted to be a musician. In 1960, he graduated from Fisk University with a B.A. in English

51

and became politically active in the civil rights movement. He also pursued his music interests—writing songs, singing, and playing the guitar, banjo, clarinet, and piano. In the late 60s, Lester moved to New York City where he hosted and produced a radio show on WBAI-FM for eight years and a live television show on WNET for two years. During this time he also published a number of books for adults. With the advice of his publisher, Lester started writing children's books. His advice for someone who wants to be a writer is to read, read, read. It is important to know what others have written. It is important to learn the possibilities of things to write about and the ways to write about them. According to Lester, there is no substitute for reading everything you can get your hands on.

Discussion Questions

- Was the story realistic?
- Were the characters fictional or actual persons?
- Did the story accurately represent the time period?
- Did you learn more about life during these times from reading this book?
- Was the main character strong-willed? Give examples.
- Two characters told this story. Who were they, and did the change in the point of view add to or detract from the story?
- Was the ending as you expected or different?
- Describe the mood of this story.

Content Area Connections

Language Arts

Students may:

- Create a diary for one of the characters in the story. Continue the story from the book as they wish, making changes to the circumstances and the character's personality as they see fit. Be sure to remain true to the time period.
- Create a "story star" for potential readers. Make it a five-pointed star. In the center, put "Why?" and write the author's theme for the story. At one point put "When?" and tell when the story took place and describe the mood. At another point put "What happened?" and briefly tell the important events of the story. At another point put "Who?" and write a brief description of the main characters. At another point put "Where?" and tell the setting of the story. At the last point, put "Recommend?" and write their recommendation for the potential reader about the book. Or they could put "Resolution?" and write the ending of the story if they wish.

Social Studies

Students may:

- Compare the timeline (events and characters) depicted in this story to the timeline in a social studies text chapter about life in Ancient Egypt.

Art

Students may:

- Create their name in hieroglyphs on a piece of tag paper for their desk.

Technology

Students may:

- Create a travel brochure for Ancient Egypt. Include pictures and information about the Nile, the pyramids, and the temples. Include some decorative hieroglyphs.

Mapping

Students may:

- Create a K-W-L chart about life in Ancient Egypt. Make three columns on their paper. For KNOW (K), list all the things they know; for WANT TO KNOW (W), list the things they would like to know more about. At the end of their exploration and discovery, they can fill in the LEARNED (L) column with the additional information they learned.

Snack: Figs, dates, pomegranates, grapes

Annotated Titles About Ancient Egypt

Aliki. *Mummies Made in Egypt.* Thomas Y. Crowell Co., 1987.
Aliki describes and illustrates the techniques of mummification and explains the reasons for using it in Ancient Egypt.

Andronik, Catherine. *Hatshepsut, His Majesty, Herself.* Atheneum Books for Young Readers, 2001.
An excellent picture book, it describes the life of Hatshepsut, a woman who was queen and then named herself pharaoh and ruled for twenty years in Ancient Egypt.

Berger, Melvin and Gilda. *Mummies of the Pharaohs: Exploring the Valley of the Kings.* National Geographic Society, 2001.
This is a retelling of Howard Carter's discovery of King Tutankhamun's tomb.

It includes beautiful color photographs of actual artifacts from the tomb and a section on the great tomb of Pharaoh Seti I.

Bower, Tamara. *The Shipwrecked Sailor: An Egyptian Tale with Hieroglyphs.* Atheneum Books for Young Readers, 2000.

"This story is found in an ancient papyrus scroll in the Pushkin Museum in Moscow." This nineteenth century B.C. story tells of a sailor who is shipwrecked on the Island of Soul along with a serpent who is the Prince of Punt. The serpent foretells the sailor's rescue and gives him many gifts so he can return to his family. Highlighted text is retold in hieroglyphs.

Bunting, Eve. *I Am the Mummy: Heb-Nefert.* Harcourt, Brace and Co., 1997.

The mummy Heb-Nefert recalls her life in ancient Egypt as the privileged wife of the pharaoh's brother. She preceded her husband in death and was anointed, bound in linen, and placed in her sarcophagus along with her beloved cat, Nebut.

Carter, Dorothy Sharp. *His Majesty: Queen Hatshepsut.* Lippincott, Williams & Wilkins Publishers, 1987.

Hatshepsut, a thirteen-year-old Egyptian princess, doesn't feel she is entirely fortunate. After all, she is a girl. But Hatshepsut little knows what life has in store for her. By the time she is fourteen years old, she will be a wife and shortly thereafter, a queen. The early death of her husband makes Hatshepsut Queen-Regent, ruling jointly with her husband's son—a son who is only a child, and the child of a concubine at that. Hatshepsut thrives as Queen-Regent, creating opportunities to act for the good of her people and the glory of Egypt. Yet she chafes at sharing her reign with a child. Seizing the supreme opportunity, Hatshepsut names herself Pharaoh, setting aside the young heir to the throne. She rules as King of Upper and Lower Egypt for more than twenty years.

Climo, Shirley. *The Egyptian Cinderella.* HarperCollins, 1989.

A retelling of an ancient Egyptian version of Cinderella features Rhodopis, who is devastated when a falcon swoops down and steals one of her precious red slippers until the Pharaoh uses it as a clue to find his bride.

Cooney, Caroline. *Mummy.* Scholastic Incorporated, 2000.

Emlyn is a model student and a great athlete—a girl who doesn't seem to have a dark side. But secretly she's always wondered what it would be like to commit a crime and get away with it. When she gets involved in a prank to steal a mummy, everything goes according to plan. Until Emlyn is forced to save the mummy—and herself.

Frank, John. *The Tomb of the Boy King.* Farrar Straus Giroux, 2001.

In poetry format, John Frank tells of the discovery in the Valley of the Kings of the tomb of the boy king Tutankhamen, who was only eighteen years old when he died or was murdered. Although Howard Carter found over 5,000 objects in the tomb, the backer of the project may have suffered from the fatal Tutankhamen curse.

Gregory, Kristina. *Cleopatra VII: Daughter of the Nile.* Scholastic Incorporated, 1999.

Cleopatra is only twelve years old when the book begins in Egypt, 57 B.C. Her father is in hiding after a deadly puff-adder snake was found in his chambers, and Tryphaena, the eldest daughter, has declared herself the queen. Cleopatra and her father, King Ptolemy Auletes, fear for their lives. They flee Egypt and sail to Rome to ask for help and troops from Julius Caesar. King Ptolemy thinks only about himself and his pleasures; thus both the Romans and the Egyptians have lost respect for him and he is openly ridiculed. In spite of this, Cleopatra must be cautious of the King: "He can be gentle and loving, but if threatened, he will kill." Thoughtfully and carefully she must prepare herself to be queen. Part of the Royal Diaries series.

Leviathan, David, adaptor. *The Mummy.* Scholastic Incorporated, 1999.

A junior novelization of the movie *The Mummy*, a story about an adventurer named Rick O'Connell and a daring librarian, Evelyn Carnahan, who team up to search for an ancient Egyptian artifact. During their search they accidentally resurrect the mummy of the High Priest, Imhotep.

Macaulay, David. *Pyramid.* Houghton Mifflin Company, 1982.

Detailed pen-and-ink drawings enhance the story of what many think was the way ancient pyramids were actually constructed. Macaulay takes the reader through the process, from selecting and preparing the piece of land through the entombment of the pharaoh. There is a glossary of Egyptian terms.

Mann, Elizabeth. *The Great Pyramid.* Mikaya Press, 1996.

In 2550 B.C., Khufu took the throne in Egypt and declared himself to be the greatest pharaoh. He built a tomb on the Giza Plateau, a 50-story, 13-acre pyramid. This great pyramid still stands 4,500 years later.

Meltzer, Milton. *In the Days of the Pharaohs: A Look at Ancient Egypt.* Franklin Watts, 2001.

The topics include the Nile, pharaohs, laws, wars, pyramids, gods, mummies, inventions, hieroglyphs, food, and women. There are black-and-white and color photographs.

Millard, Anne. *Pyramids.* Kingfisher, 1996.

After an initial focus on Egyptian pyramids, the author discusses pyramids from around the world, explaining the purpose, shape, construction, and significance of pyramids in various cultures.

Snyder, Zilpha Keatley. *The Egypt Game.* Yearling Books, 1986.

The first time Melanie Ross meets April Hall, she's not sure they'll have anything in common. But she soon discovers they both love anything to do with ancient Egypt. When they stumble upon a deserted storage yard behind the A-Z Antiques and Curio Shop, Melanie and April decide it's the perfect spot for the Egypt Game. Before long there are six Egyptians instead of two. After school and on weekends they all meet to wear costumes, hold ceremonies, and work on their secret code. Everyone thinks it's just a game until strange things begin happening to the players. Has the Egypt Game gone too far?

Additional Titles About Ancient Egypt

Atlas of Ancient Egypt. McGraw-Hill Children's Publishing, 2000.

Caselli, Giovanni. *In Search of Tutankhamen: The Discovery of a King's Tomb.* Peter Bedrick Books, 1999.

Cooney, Caroline. *For All Time.* Delacorte Press, 2001.

Curry, Jane Louise. *The Egyptian Box.* Margaret K. McElderry, 2002.

Donoughue, Carol. *The Mystery of the Hieroglyphs: The Story of the Rosetta Stone and the Race to Decipher Egyptian Hieroglyphs.* Oxford University Press, 1999.

Giblin, James C. *The Riddle of the Rosetta Stone: Key to Ancient Egypt.* Harper-Collins Children's Book Group, 1990.

Green, Robert. *Tutankhamen.* Franklin Watts, 1996.

Hart, George. *Ancient Egypt.* Alfred A. Knopf, 1990.

Haynes, Joyce. *Egyptian Dynasties.* Franklin Watts, 1998.

Karr, Kathleen. *Bone Dry.* Hyperion Books for Young Readers, 2002.

Landau, Elaine. *The Curse of the Tutankhamen.* Millbrook Press Inc., 1996.

Lauber, Patricia. *Tales Mummies Tell.* Thomas Y. Crowell, 1985.

Pemberton, Delia. *Egyptian Mummies: People from the Past.* Harcourt Children's Books, 2001.

Pickels, Dwayne E. *Egyptian Kings and Queens and Classical Deities.* Chelsea House Publishers, 1997.

Remler, Pat. *Egyptian Mythology A to Z: A Young Reader's Companion.* Facts on File, 2000.

Rubalcaba, Jill. *A Place in the Sun.* Houghton Mifflin Company, 1997.

Steedman, Scott. *The Egyptian News.* Candlewick Press, 1997.

Trumble, Kelly. *Cat Mummies.* Clarion Books, 1996.

Wood, Tim. *Ancient Wonders.* Viking Press, 1997.

Annotated Titles by Julius Lester

Ackamarackus: Julius Lester's Sumptuously Silly Fantastically Funny Fables. Scholastic Trade, 2001.

Readers of all ages will laugh at these irresistible creatures and their gleefully absurd predicaments, all the while unwittingly gathering wisdom about acceptance, ingenuity, and individuality.

Albidaro and the Mischievous Dream. Phyllis Fogelman Books, 2000.

The children of the world are tired of doing what they're told. A mischievous dream whispers to them that they should stop listening to their parents. But it doesn't end there. Next the dream visits all the animals and tells them they should do whatever they want, too. Soon animals are invading fine restaurants, taking up all the space on the couch, and leaving the water on when they get out of the shower. Can Albidaro, Guardian of Children, and Olara, Guardian of Animals, put everyone back where they're supposed to be?

The Blues Singers: Ten Who Rocked the World, Jump at the Sun, 2001.
A picture-book tribute to ten blues singers is told by a grandfather to his grand-daughter. Each description contains factual information about the artist plus a personal vignette about Lester's connection to the artist. The book includes a bibliography and a list of recommended listening.

From Slave Ship to Freedom Road. Dial Books, 1998.
Magnificent paintings by artist Rod Brown coupled with the meditations of Julius Lester make this a stirring testimony to the strength and endurance of the slaves, their ancestors.

John Henry. Dial Books for Young Readers, 1994.
A clever retelling of an African American folk ballad with humor, energy, and tall-tale charm.

Long Journey Home: Stories from Black History. Puffin Books, 1998.
This book contains six stories of slavery based on actual people and events.

Othello: A Novel. Point, 1998.
This is an interpretation of Shakespeare's classic story of Othello, with Othello, Desdemona, and Iago cast as African Americans in Elizabethan England.

Sam and the Tigers: A New Telling of Little Black Sambo. Puffin Books, 2000.
Little Black Sambo by Helen Bannerman is re-created in a Black Southern storytelling voice. The storyteller turns Sam's deals with hungry tigers into an exciting contest of wits and his pancake dinner into a feast for the whole community.

To Be a Slave. Puffin Books, 2000.
A collection of the memories of slaves and ex-slaves as they tell of their trials and tribulations, starting with leaving Africa through the Civil War and into the twentieth century.

What a Truly Cool World. Scholastic Trade, 1999.
A creation story in which God walks around in bedroom slippers and has a wife named Iren and a secretary named Bruce. God's chair is a recliner, and the story is told in Lester's favorite Black storytelling voice.

Teacher Resources About Ancient Egypt

Applegate, Melissa Littlefield. *The Egyptian Book of Life.* Health Communications, 2000.
Breyer, Michelle. *Ancient Egypt Interdisciplinary Unit.* Teacher Created Materials, 1996.
Brown, Karen and Holly Engel. *Read and Respond: Ancient Egypt Literature.* Edupress Publishing, 1994.
Hamilton, Robyn. *Ancient Egypt Activity Book.* Edupress Publishing, 1990.
Hotle, Patrick. *Egypt and the Middle East.* Mark Twain Media, Inc., 1995.
Milton, Joyce. *Hieroglyphs.* Grosset & Dunlap, 2000.
Pofahl, Jane. *Ancient Civilizations: Egypt.* T.S. Denison & Company, Inc., 1993.

Sterling, Mary Ellen. *Ancient Egypt Thematic Unit.* Teacher Created Materials, 1992.

Sylvester, Diane. *Egypt, Kush, and Aksum.* Frank Schaffer Publications, 1997.

Wassynger, Ruth Akamine. *Ancient Egypt.* Scholastic Professional Books, 1996.

Wyma, Brenda. *Ancient Egypt.* Creative Teaching Press, 1992.

Web Sites About Ancient Egypt

A Pyramid Puzzle
http://wcvt.com/~tiggr/
Guardian's Egypt: Pyramids
http://www.guardians.net/egypt/pyramids.htm
Construction of Pyramids
http://interoz.com/egypt/construction/construc.htm
Guardian's Giza Plateau
http://www.guardians.net/egypt/giza1.htm
Pyramids of Giza
http://www.pbs.org/wgbh/nova/pyramid/
NOVA Pyramids: The Inside Story
http://library.thinkquest.org/10098/egypt.htm
Egyptian Mathematics: Numbers
http://www.eyelid.co.uk/numbers.htm
Mark Millmore's Ancient Egypt
http://www.eyelid.co.uk/index.htm

Web Sites About Julius Lester

Meet Authors and Illustrators
http://www.childrenslit.com/f_lester.html
Meet the Author: Julius Lester
http://www.eduplace.com/kids/hmr/mtai/lester.html
The Bulletin of the Center for Children's Books: True Blue—Julius Lester
http://alexia.lis.uiuc.edu/puboff/bccb/1099true.html
Questions & Answers with Julius Lester
http://wildes.home.mindspring.com/OUAL/int/lesterjulius.html
Julius Lester
http://dept.kent.edu/virginiahamiltonconf/lester.htm
Interview with Julius Lester at Amazon.com
http://www.amazon.com/exec/obidos/show-interview/l-j-esterulius/
103-0985017-1568642

Contact Publisher:

Silver Whistle/Harcourt
15 East 26th Street
New York, NY 10010

8

Rowan of Rin by Emily Rodda (Greenwillow Books, 2001)

Genre: Fantasy
Theme: Dragons and Quests

Introduction

Set the tone for this book club session by dressing up as you would to go on a long and difficult journey. Begin the discussion by asking what you need to bring both physically and mentally to survive such a journey. Then launch into a discussion of *Rowan of Rin* and the Australian author Emily Rodda. Topics to explore are Australia, Australian Authors Children's Book Awards, famous journeys and explorers, dragons, and the concepts of bravery and heroes both past and present.

Summary of *Rowan of Rin*

Rowan will never be the man his father was—or will he? Rowan tended the bukshah, the special gentle animals that graze near the water that flows from the nearby mountain. One day the water stopped flowing and the daily roar of the dragon was heard no more. The people of Rin decide someone must go up the mountain to find out what is stopping the water from flowing down the mountain. Several men and women volunteer and they decide to consult with Sheba, who some consider either a witch or a wise woman. Sheba warns them that the mountain has ways of taming and destroying the bravest among them. She leaves them with a riddle and a strange map that is visible only when being held by Rowan, thus ensuring his participation in the journey up the mountain. Sheba's words ring in their ears: "Seven hearts the journey make./ Seven ways the hearts will break." Rowan, the youngest and most afraid, would face the dragon alone and prove to be brave, wise, and strong.

Information About Emily Rodda

Emily Rodda has written many books for children, including *Finders Keepers,* which *School Library Journal* dubbed a lively adventure, and several novels about the likable hero Rowan. The first of these novels, *Rowan of Rin,* won the Children's Book Council of Australia Book of the Year for Younger Readers Award when it was first published. In fact, Emily Rodda has won the Children's Book Council of Australia Book of the Year Award an unprecedented five times. A former editor, Ms. Rodda is also a best-selling author of adult mysteries under the name Jennifer Rowe. She lives in Australia.

Discussion Questions

- What makes this book different from other books you have read?
- Were you able to imagine what a bukshah looked like?
- Why is Rowan an unlikely candidate to visit the dragon?
- Do you think the clues added to the story?
- How would you describe a hero?
- Did you feel you were part of this story or only observing?
- Was the description adequate for you to picture what was happening?
- Who is the most interesting character?
- Did you dislike any of the characters? If so, which one?

Content Area Connections

Language Arts

Students may:

- Write a poem about a dragon and illustrate it.
- Write a story about what might happen if a dragon were discovered today.
- Write a story about a quest to find something; change the story of Rowan to reflect a similar journey but in modern times or the future; or change the ending.

Social Studies

Students may:

- Research dragons. When and where were they thought to exist?

Science

Students may:

- Research why the Komodo Dragon is called a dragon when it is really a lizard. What characteristics does it have that possibly led to that name?

Art

Students may:

- Create a map with directions to a treasure guarded by a dragon.
- Design a flowchart of events from the story *Rowan of Rin.*

Mapping

Students may:

- Create a concept map about dragons. Put the word dragon in the center and make the second layer appearance, breathing, habitat, diet, skin, and personality. On the third layer, write as many words as they can think of that describe a dragon.

Technology

Students may:

- Research famous journeys on the Internet. Create a chart of some famous explorers and what they found.

Snack: Trail mix, granola bars, rocky road fudge

Annotated Titles About Dragons and Quests

Base, Graeme. *The Discovery of Dragons.* Harry N. Abrams, Inc., 1996.

Victorian scientist R.W. Greasebeam presents a series of letters—by a ninth-century Viking, a thirteenth-century Chinese girl, and a Prussian cartographer, among others—and colorful artwork recording the discovery of the world's most fearsome dragons.

Calabro, Marian. *The Perilous Journey of the Donner Party.* Clarion Books, 1999.

Life was good for the well-off Donner and Reed families in Springfield, Illinois. The prospect of large tracts of land in California 2500 miles away sounded appealing. They packed up all they owned and left April 15, 1846. They joined with another group that eventually totaled 87 people. Under the influence of James Reed they took the Hastings Cutoff, which was supposed to shorten the journey by 300 miles. The trail was nonexistent, so they cut a wagon trail through the Wasatch Mountains in Utah. Instead of covering 12–15 miles per day, they covered only 2–5 miles. As a result they reached the Sierra Nevada summit, Truckee Lake (now Donner Lake) in late October. They were unable to cross the summit because of weather, hunger, and fatigue. Eighty-one people were forced to make camp at Truckee Lake and try to survive the winter until help could come. They were desperate people and took desperate measures to survive. Virginia Reed, age thirteen, wrote later to her cousin, "O Mary I have not rote you half of the truble we have had but I have rote you anuf to let you now that you don't know what truble is. . . . Don't let this letter dishaten [dishearten] anybody never take no cut-ofs and hury along as fast as you can." Forty-seven survivors reached California.

Coville, Bruce. *Jeremy Thatcher, Dragon Hatcher.* Harcourt Children's Books, 1991.
Jeremy visits a magic shop one afternoon and becomes the owner of a dragon egg. Next thing he knows, he is raising a tiny dragon named Tiamat. The dragon is impish and grows quickly. Soon Jeremy realizes he can no longer keep his friend.

Deedy, Carmen Agra. *The Library Dragon.* Peachtree Press, 1994.
Sunrise Elementary School has a big problem. Their new librarian, Miss Lotta Scales, was "a real dragon." Miss Lotta is so consumed with her responsibility to the books that she is determined not to let any children near them. "She kept a fiery eye out to make sure no one removed any books from the shelves.... The very thought of sticky little fingers touching and clutching, pawing and clawing, smearing and tearing her precious books just made her hot under the collar."

Grahame, Kenneth. *The Reluctant Dragon.* Holiday House, 1938.
This is a classic story about the Boy who was allowed to read as much as he liked and was fond of natural history and fairy tales. When his father, a sheepherder, dis-covers a dragon's cave, it is the Boy who meets the dragon. This is no ordinary dragon. This dragon is quiet, shy, retiring, and makes up poetry verses. The Boy's worst fears come true. St. George is on his way to slay this reluctant dragon.

Hague, Michael. *The Book of Dragons.* William Morrow & Company, 1995.
Michael Hague has collected seventeen dragon stories from authors such as C.S. Lewis, Kenneth Grahame, J.R.R. Tolkien, and E. Nesbit. These stories are ac-companied by numerous color and black-and-white illustrations.

Munsch, Robert. *The Paper Bag Princess.* Annick Press, 1988.
The Princess Elizabeth is planning her wedding to Prince Ronald when a dragon attacks the castle and kidnaps Ronald. So Elizabeth goes off and finds the dragon, outsmarts him, and finally rescues Ronald. But Ronald is not too happy to see Princess Elizabeth looking dirty and disheveled. Then doesn't he get a sur-prise!

Park, Linda Sue. *A Single Shard.* Clarion Books, 2001.
A Single Shard is a humble story of perseverance, patience, and courage. The story takes place during the twelfth century in a potter's village in Korea. Tree-ear was orphaned at a young age and was brought to the village of Ch'ulp'o to live with an uncle. When Tree-ear arrived, the uncle died of the fever and Tree-ear was brought to Crane-man, who was to take care of him temporarily. Tree-ear re-mained with Crane-man, and they lived under the bridge, surviving by their wiles and frugalness. Tree-ear was fascinated by the potter Min and observed

him, unbeknownst to Min. One day when Tree-ear was bold enough to pick up one of the unfired pieces, Min startled him and the boy dropped the piece. Thus began a debt that led to Tree-ear's working long and hard for Min with hopes of becoming a potter one day. The journey is long: "One hill, one valley…one day at a time."

Rupp, Rebecca. *The Dragon of Lonely Island.* Candlewick Press, 1998.
Great Aunt Mehitabel had a vacation house on remote Lonely Island in Maine. The Davis children and their mother were going to spend the summer there. Aunt Mehitabel would not be there, so she sent the children a key to the tower room and suggested that they explore Drake's Hill. The children learn that drake is an ancient name for dragon. The children discover a peaceful tridrake that has three heads and three tales to tell the children.

Seabrooke, Brenda. *The Care and Feeding of Dragons.* Cobblehill Books, 1998.
Alistair's parents will allow him to keep his little blue dragon, Spike, if he can take care of it and keep his grades up. Alistair is starting fourth grade and has the dreaded Ms. Cassowary for a teacher. The first day of school, Alistair is assigned a one-page paper to write for climbing in the window of his class and falling at the feet of Ms. Cassowary. When he returns home, Spike doesn't seem to be breathing and was unhappy about being alone. Alistair doesn't know how he will survive the year.

Wilson, Diane Lee. *I Rode a Horse of Milk White Jade.* Orchard Books, 1998.
Oyuna was born on the Mongolian steppes during the reign of Kublai Khan (1339). When she is still an infant, Oyuna's foot is crushed by a horse and her clan believes she is cursed with bad luck. At thirteen, Oyuna sets off on a journey disguised as a boy, taking her white mare and her cat. Oyuna has a special gift with horses and can hear her mare speak (sometimes). She goes in search of the perfect white horse belonging to Kublai Khan so she can win a race. The story is told by an elderly Oyuna to her granddaughter as they await the birth of a foal—a direct descendent of Oyuna's beloved mare in the story.

Yolen, Jane. *Here There Be Dragons.* Harcourt Brace & Company, 1993.
Jane Yolen introduces each of her poems and stories about dragons with an insight as to what inspired her to write it. Some of the work was published previously, but many of the poems and stories are new. The last entry in the book is "Here There Be Dragons."

———. *Merlin and the Dragons.* Cobblehill Books, 1995.
Young Arthur has a recurring dream about a fatherless boy who becomes a king simply by pulling a sword from a stone. Merlin comforts the boy with a story about another fatherless boy who dreams about dragons and his dreams, which come true. This wondrously illustrated picture book introduces the legendary King Arthur and Merlin.

Additional Titles About Dragons and Quests

Auch, Mary Jane. *Journey to Nowhere.* Henry Holt and Company, 1997.

Bauer, Joan. *Rules of the Road.* Putnam Publishing Group, 1999.

Buss, Fran L. *Journey of the Sparrows.* Penguin Putnam Books for Young Readers, 1991.

Coville, Bruce. *The Dragonslayers.* Simon & Schuster Children's Publishing, 1994.

Creech, Sharon. *Walk Two Moons.* HarperCollins Publishers, 1994.

Fletcher, Susan. *Dragon's Milk.* Atheneum Publications, 1989.

———. *Flight of the Dragon.* Atheneum Publications, 1993.

———. *Sign of the Dove.* Atheneum Publications, 1996.

Gray, Luli. *Falcon and the Charles Street Witch.* Houghton Mifflin Company, 2002.

———. *Falcon's Egg.* Ticknor & Fields Books for Young Readers, 1995.

Ibbotson, Eva. *Journey to the River Sea.* Penguin Putnam Books for Young Readers, 2002.

Jordan, Sheryl. *The Hunting of the Last Dragon.* HarperCollins Children's Book Group, 2002.

McCaffrey, Anne. *A Diversity of Dragons.* Atheneum Books for Young Readers, 1995.

Paulsen, Gary. *The Car.* Harcourt Children's Books, 1994.

Seabrooke, Brenda. *The Dragon That Ate Summer.* Penguin Putnam, Incorporated, 1992.

Sterman, Betsy and Samuel. *Backyard Dragon.* HarperCollins Children's Book Group, 1993.

Stewart, Jennifer J. *If That Breathes Fire, We're Toast.* Holiday House, 1999.

Stewart, Sarah. *The Journey.* Farrar Straus Giroux, 2001.

Takai, Ronald. *Journey to Golden Mountain: The Chinese in Nineteenth Century America.* Chelsea House Publishers, 1994.

Wrede, Patricia C. *Dealing with Dragons.* Harcourt Brace Jovanovich, 1990.

———. *Searching for Dragons.* Harcourt Children's Books, 1991.

Yolen, Jane. *Dragon's Blood: A Fantasy.* Delacorte Press, 1982.

———. *Dragon's Boy.* Harper & Row, 1990.

———. *Heart's Blood.* Delacorte Press, 1984.

———. *The Sending of Dragons.* Harcourt Brace and Company, 1987.

Zhang, Song Nan. *A Time of Golden Dragons.* Tundra Books of Northern New York, 2000.

Annotated Titles by Emily Rodda

Deltora Quest: City of the Rats. Apple, 2001.

Lief, Barda, and Jasmine continue on their journey to find all seven stones in the magic belt of Deltora. They are empowered by the first two gems as they travel to their destination of the City of Rats, where they will search for the third gem while trying to battle the city's horrors.

Deltora Quest: Deltora Book of Monsters. Scholastic Incorporated, 2002.
This book tells the history of Deltora and all the creatures. McBride's fantasy art is superb.

Deltora Quest: Dread Mountain. Apple, 2001.
Lief, Barda, and Jasmine travel to the evil Dread Mountain to try to find the fifth gem in the magic belt of Deltora.

Deltora Quest: The Lake of Tears. Apple, 2001.
Lief and Barda have a new friend as they begin a treacherous journey through the territory ruled by the monster sorceress Thaegan. They have a difficult task: They must face the horrible guardian of the Lake of Tears to obtain the second gem.

Deltora Quest: The Valley of the Lost. Apple, 2001.
This is the seventh book in the Deltora Quest series. Lief, Barda, and Jasmine have almost completed their quest of finding all seven gems in the magic belt of Deltora. Now the seventh gem must be found before the Shadow Lord will free Deltora. The friends have faced amazing dangers in the past, but this will be the worst, and if they do not succeed, they will be forever ensnared in the mists of the Valley of the Lost.

Rowan and the Keeper of the Crystal. Greenwillow Books, 2002.
In this third book of the Rowan stories, Rowan's mother is poisoned and falls into a deep sleep. She is unable to select the new keeper of the crystal, which is her ancestral duty. Rowan decides to defy tradition and find the antidote before assuming her duties. He takes the three candidates for keeper with him as he searches for the antidote. He encounters a deadly sea serpent and is required to solve a mysterious riddle along the way.

Rowan and the Travelers. Greenwillow Books, 2002.
In this sequel to *Rowan of Rin,* Rowan tries to understand a mysterious sleeping sickness that causes the townspeople to fall into an enchanted sleep. This all started when a nomadic tribe called the Travelers came to town. Rowan and a girl Traveler, Zeel, enter the legendary noxious Pit of Unrin to try to discover the secret of the sleeping sickness.

Rowan and the Zebak. Greenwillow Books, 2002.
In this further tale in the saga of Rowan of Rin, Rowan has a premonition of a pending disaster but does nothing. His younger sister, Annad, is kidnapped by a flying grach and taken to the land of the Zebak. Rowan feels responsible for this tragedy. Armed with directions from the local witch, Sheba, Rowan embarks with three friends on a journey to find his sister.

Web Sites About Dragons

At The Edge—Dragons of the Marches
http://www.indigogroup.co.uk/edge/dragons.htm

D.R.A.G.O.N.S.
http://www.colba.net/~tempest1/dragons.htm
Dragons & Serpents in Sussex
http://www2.prestel.co.uk/aspen/sussex/dragon.html
Dragons in Ancient China
http://www.chinapage.com/dragon1.html
Dragons of the British Isles
http://www.wyrm.demon.co.uk/ukdracs.htm
Dragons of the World—European Dragons
http://www.igolddragon.com/europeandragons.htm
Here Be Dragons
http://www.draconian.com/home/frameset.htm
Historical Dragon Page
http://members.tripod.com/~gfriebe/drach.htm

Web Sites About Emily Rodda

Emily Rodda's Web Site
http://www.emilyrodda.com
Interview with Emily Rodda
http://www.harpercollins.com/catalog/book_interview_xml.asp?
isbn = 0064410196
Emily Rodda Profile
http://www.scholastic.com.au/Profiles/ProfileDisplay.asp?
ProfileId = 60

Contact Publisher:

Greenwillow/HarperCollins
10 East 53rd Street
New York, NY 10022

9

William Shakespeare: His Work and His World by Michael Rosen and illustrated by Robert Ingpen (Candlewick Press, 2002)

Genre: Biography
Theme: William Shakespeare

Introduction

Introduce this book club topic with music typical of this era, and give a short synopsis of what life was like during this time period and the influence it might have had on William Shakespeare. This topic would be especially useful if book club members read this book in conjunction with studying one of Shakespeare's plays. Use excerpts from videos of Shakespeare's plays or, if possible, take your students to see a local production of Shakespeare. Numerous topics to discuss are the Globe Theater, history of theater, Shakespeare's life, his writings, and his legacy.

Summary of *William Shakespeare: His Work and His World*

A dramatic account of the overnight removal of an entire London playhouse gives this book a great start. Rosen then delves into the theater, culture, and daily life in Elizabethan times and includes some interesting tidbits about Shakespeare's personal life. He also closely examines four of Shakespeare's better-known plays with special emphasis on the language used by Shakespeare. The illustrations add a great deal to the text. The book includes a useful timeline and a very complete bibliography.

Information About Michael Rosen

If he weren't already a poet, storyteller, BBC broadcaster, and children's book author, Michael Rosen says he would like to be an actor.

Anyone who has seen him in performance knows he already is—whether bringing his humorous verse to life in front of a classroom or presenting an internationally broadcast radio show.

The charismatic author was introduced to the pleasures of language at an early age by his parents, both of them distinguished educators in London, England. When he was a teenager, his mother produced a British radio program that featured poetry, and this inspired him to start writing his own. Now a highly popular children's poet and author, Michael Rosen is known for "telling it like it is" in the ordinary language children actually use. In the picture book *This Is Our House,* his first book with Candlewick Press, he captures the ways children use the language of discrimination. "Our attitudes about who's okay and who's not okay get formed when we're very young," says the author, whose simple, lighthearted story makes a compelling case for tolerance.

Michael Rosen spends an enormous amount of time in schools, working with children. When putting together *Classic Poetry: An Illustrated Collection,* he selected poems he knew firsthand that children would appreciate, together with biographical sketches of the poets themselves. "There are so many ways to enjoy poems," the author says. "This book is a way of offering new insights into poems, poets, and the relationship between them…to show that great poems have been written by real people who lived in their own time and place."

The idea that great writing comes from real people who are influenced by a certain time and place is key to the appeal of *Shakespeare: His Work and His World,* a delightful, engaging look at a literary icon that asks, "What's so special about Shakespeare?" For his rich insight on the topic, Michael Rosen can again thank his parents. "When I was a kid, I was often taken to see Shakespeare's plays, and my parents helped me get hold of what was special about Shakespeare," he says. "I've written this book in hopes that I can do something along the lines of what my parents did for me."

Michael Rosen lives in London, England.

Information About Robert Ingpen, Illustrator

Robert Ingpen has created numerous books for children and adults. He has received the Hans Christian Andersen Medal for international children's illustrations and the Dromkeen Medal for his contribution to illustration in Australia. He and his wife, Angela, have four children and four grandchildren. He says, "As I designed and refined my illustrations for Tom Pow's beautiful poem, *Who Is the World For?*, I kept in mind editor

Wendy Boase, who passed away last year. Through the picture books she has published, the world is a better place."

Discussion Questions

- Was the organization of this book effective?
- How does this book compare to or contrast with other books about Shakespeare?
- Do the illustrations help you understand Shakespeare's life and times?
- How does the information in this book compare to what you already knew about Shakespeare?
- Was there anything unusual about the style of this book?
- Did you find the timeline helpful?
- Did you find that the variety in print size added to or detracted from the overall understanding of the book?
- What is your favorite quotation from Shakespeare's plays?
- What would you like to ask the author and the illustrator of this book?
- Were there parts of the book you did not understand? If so, what puzzled you?

Content Area Connections

Language Arts

Students may:

- Write a Shakespearean sonnet.
- Create a newspaper front page with headlines and stories from Shakespeare's time.
- Read through quotations from Shakespeare's plays in *Bartlett's Book of Familiar Quotations* and write down and share the ones they are most surprised to learn are from Shakespeare.

Social Studies

Students may:

- Research Shakespeare's home town of Stratford-upon-Avon and make a map showing the important landmarks.
- Research Shakespearean theaters like the Globe—make a Venn diagram to compare and contrast the theater in those days with Broadway of today.
- Create a Shakespeare trivia game.

Science

Students may:

• Research bubonic plague (Black Death), a serious disease in Shakespeare's times. Find out how many it killed, what medicines were used to treat it, and if it could happen today. Prepare to present their information in a report to the class.

Art

Students may:

• Create a poster to advertise the book.

Technology

Students may:

• Research the Globe Theater on the Internet and create presentations for the class with all that they discover—both past and present—about this famous theater.

Mapping

Students may:

• Find as much information about Shakespeare's family as they can and create a family tree—they will find he has no direct-line descendants.

Snack: Scones, tea, strawberries, cucumber sandwiches

Annotated Titles About William Shakespeare

Aliki. *William Shakespeare and the Globe.* HarperCollins Publishers, 1999.
This is the story of William Shakespeare and the Globe Theater taken from information gathered from the history of the sixteenth and seventeenth centuries: places where he lived, his plays and poems, and legal documents and drawings. Richly illustrated.

Blackwood, Gary. *The Shakespeare Stealer.* Dutton Children's Books, 1998.
This historical fiction is about the Elizabethan Age and the famous Globe Theater. Widget is a fourteen-year-old orphan who has an apprenticeship with Mr. Bright, who teaches him a form of shorthand. His next master sends him to London to steal the script of the "Tragedy of Hamlet, Prince of Denmark," so it can be performed without paying royalties. However, when Widget goes to London, a whole new world opens up to him.

Chrisp, Peter, *Shakespeare.* Dorling Kindersley, 2002.
This is a DK Eyewitness Book filled with pictures depicting Shakespeare's life. It begins with Shakespeare's birthplace and follows his life and the times as he

grows up. It includes information on costumes, comedies, tragedies, Shakespeare as an actor and writer, and his legacy. It's an excellent resource for information about Shakespeare presented in a clear and organized format.

Cooper, Susan. *King of Shadows.* Margaret K. McElderry, 1999.

Nat Field's short life has been shadowed by loss, but he is thrilled to be selected by an international director to perform at Shakespeare's Globe—London's amazing 400-year-old theater. While rehearsing in London, Nat becomes very ill. He travels back in time to 1599 and performs at the Globe Theater along with Shakespeare. He develops a close relationship with Shakespeare and is devastated to leave him when he returns to the present. He discovers that the switch was necessary because the "other" Nat Field had bubonic plague, and if he hadn't left, Shakespeare would have contracted the disease and died.

Garfield, Leon. *Shakespeare Stories II.* Houghton Mifflin Company, 1995.

This companion volume to *Shakespeare Stories* includes nine of Shakespeare's plays in a narrative format. The author includes Shakespeare's own language in the retelling. The contents include *Much Ado About Nothing, Julius Caesar, Antony and Cleopatra, Measure for Measure, As You Like It, Cymbeline, King Richard the Third, The Comedy of Errors,* and *The Winter's Tale.*

Langley, Andrew. *Shakespeare's Theatre.* Oxford University Press, 1999.

American filmmaker and actor Sam Wanamaker fulfilled a dream to rebuild Shakespeare's Globe Theatre in almost the same spot as the original. The new Globe Theatre opened in 1997 on London's River Thames after seventeen years of construction, copying the original techniques and materials of the 1600s. This book chronicles the history of the original Globe and its construction as well as the new Globe.

Lester, Julius. *Othello: A Novel.* Scholastic Incorporated, 1995.

Just like Shakespeare, Lester borrows from the original play to write a novel. Shakespeare's Othello is described as a Moor, which defines him as being dark and swarthy. In Lester's novel, Othello is Black, as is Iago and his wife, Emilia. The issue of race is explored in Lester's novel and acts as a bridge to Shakespeare's play.

Shakespeare, William. *The Tempest.* Doubleday Books for Young Readers, 1994.

Bruce Coville retells this prose version of *The Tempest.* His mission was to present an accurate introduction to a play all children should be exposed to in hopes that they will be inspired to read the original work.

Stanley, Diane and Peter Vennema. *Bard of Avon: The Story of William Shakespeare.* Morrow Junior Books, 1992.

Diane Stanley has approached this book as a historian. Because little is known about William Shakespeare, Diane has gathered all the known facts until a pattern appears. This book follows the journey of William starting when he was five, his marriage to Anne Hathaway at eighteen, the Globe Theatre in London, and his retirement in Stratford.

Ross, Stewart. *Shakespeare and Macbeth: The Story Behind the Play*. Viking Press, 1994.

Shakespeare wrote the play *Macbeth* to please King James, who was a patron of the arts. This play was about an eleventh-century Scottish king named Macbeth who encounters witches who appeal to his ambition and predict that he will be the future king. Macbeth commits murder to ensure the prophesy comes true, and thus the violence begins.

Turk, Ruth. *The Play's the Thing*. Carolrhoda Books Incorporated, 1998.

William Shakespeare was born in the 1500s. His father was the mayor of Stratford-upon-Avon. In 1569, using the town funds, his father sponsored a rare live play performance at which young William was present. The author gleans information about the child and the adult playwright and poet William Shakespeare from the documents researchers have gathered concerning his life.

Additional Titles About William Shakespeare

Blackwood, Gary. *Shakespeare Scribe*. Dutton Children's Books, 2000.

Burdett, Lois. *Shakespeare for Kids*. Firefly Books, Ltd., 1998

Coville, Bruce. *William Shakespeare's Romeo and Juliet*. Penguin Putnam Books for Young Readers, 1999.

——.*William Shakespeare's A Midsummer Night's Dream*. Penguin Putnam Books for Young Readers, 1996.

Ferris, Julie. *Shakespeare's London: A Guide to Elizabethan London*. Houghton Mifflin Company, 2000.

Garfield, Leon. *Shakespeare Stories I*. Schocken Books, 1985.

Lamb, Charles. *Tales from Shakespeare*. Penguin Putnam Books for Young Readers, 1995.

McCaughrean, Geraldine. *Stories from Shakespeare*. Simon & Schuster Trade, 1995.

Morley, Jacqueline. *Shakespeare's Theater*. Peter Bedrick Books, 1994.

Nesbit, Edith. *The Best of Shakespeare*. Oxford University Press, 1997.

Shellard, Dominic. *William Shakespeare*. Oxford University Press, 1998.

Williams, Marcia. *Tales from Shakespeare*. Candlewick Press, 1998.

——. *Bravo, Mr. William Shakespeare*. Candlewick Press, 2000.

Plays of William Shakespeare

1589–90	*Henry VI, Part 1*
1590–91	*Henry VI, Part 2*
1590–91	*Henry VI, Part 3*
1590–94	*The Taming of the Shrew*
1592	*Richard III*
1592–94	*The Two Gentleman of Verona*
1594–96	*King John*

1595	*Love's Labour's Lost*
1595	*Richard II*
1595–96	*Romeo and Juliet*
1595–96	*A Midsummer Night's Dream*
1596–97	*The Merchant of Venice*
1596–97	*Henry IV, Part 1*
1597	*The Merry Wives of Windsor*
1598	*Henry IV, Part 2*
1598	*Much Ado About Nothing*
1599	*As You Like It*
1599	*Henry V*
1599	*Julius Caesar*
1600–01	*Hamlet*
1600–01	*Twelfth Night*
1601–02	*Troilus and Cressida*
1602–03	*All's Well That Ends Well*
1604	*Measure for Measure*
1604	*Othello*
1604–05	*King Lear*
1606	*Macbeth*
1606–07	*Anthony and Cleopatra*
1607–08	*Coriolanus*
1607–08	*Timon of Athens*
1607–08	*Pericles*
1609–10	*Cymbeline*
1610–11	*The Winter's Tale*
1611	*The Tempest*
1613	*Henry VIII*

The Poems

1592	Venus and Adonis
1592–96	The Sonnets (154)
1594	The Rape of Lucrece
1599	The Passionate Pilgrim—second edition date
1601	The Phoenix and the Turtle
1609	A Lover's Complaint

Teacher Resources About William Shakespeare

Boyce, Charles and David Allen White. *Shakespeare A to Z: The Essential Reference to His Plays, His Poems, His Life and Times, and More.* Delta, 1991.

Egan, Lorraine Hopping. *Teaching Shakespeare, Yes You Can: Fun, Easy Activities for Teaching Any Play.* Scholastic Incorporated, 1998.

Robbins, Mary Lou. *Shakespeare.* Teacher Created Materials, 1995.

Rygiel, Mary Ann. *Shakespeare Among School Children: Approaches for the Secondary Classroom.* National Council of Teachers of English, 1992.

Web Sites About William Shakespeare

Shakespeare for Kids
http://www.shakespeare4kids.com/
National Shakespeare Company—England—Shakespeare 4 Kidz
http://www.shakespeare4kidz.com/
Article from Reading Online About Shakespeare and Middle School Kids
http://www.readingonline.org/articles/katz/katz_frame.html
Shakespeare and the Globe Theatre: Then and Now—Encyclopedia Britannica
http://shakespeare.eb.com/
Shakespeare's Historic Stratford-upon-Avon
http://www.stratford-upon-avon.co.uk/soahstry.htm
Phrases from Shakespeare
http://phrases.shu.ac.uk/meanings/shakespeare.html
Shakespeare for Teachers and Students
http://falcon.jmu.edu/~ramseyil/shakes.htm#A

Web Site About Michael Rosen

http://www.candlewickpress.com/cat.asp?browse=Title&mode=book&isbn=0763615684&pix=n

Contact Publisher:

Candlewick Press
2067 Massachusetts Avenue
Cambridge, MA 02140
http://www.candlewickpress.com

10

Williwaw! by Tom Bodett (Alfred A. Knopf, 1999)

Genre: Adventure
Theme: Alaska

Introduction

Introduce your book club session with a recording from one of Tom Bodett's audiocassettes or a clip of his Motel 6 advertisement. Show a brief segment from an Alaskan travel video to establish the setting for this Alaskan adventure. The topics of weather, Alaskan wilderness, the Poles (both Arctic and Antarctic), survival, obedience, and the Exxon Valdez could be discussed and incorporated into the curriculum.

Summary of *Williwaw!*

From humorist, storyteller, author, and the voice of Motel 6 commercials, here is an exciting middle-grade adventure novel set in rural Alaska. Ivan and September Crane, ages twelve and thirteen, are left alone for a couple of weeks while their fisherman Dad is away at sea earning money for a new fishing boat. In typical adolescent fashion, they quickly proceed to ignore his only two instructions: don't run down the batteries on the portable short-wave radio, their only means of communication, and don't cross the bay to town. Through a series of bad decisions, they find themselves crossing Bag Bay in their skiff when they are suddenly overtaken by a sudden and fierce autumn storm known as a williwaw. Ivan and September must use every ounce of strength, courage, and ingenuity they possess to keep themselves afloat until help comes. Williwaw contains rich descriptions of Alaskan geography and wildlife. Its likable characters and taut suspense will keep readers riveted until the last page.

Information About Tom Bodett

Tom Bodett is a storyteller recognized for his warm, humorous style, but he is perhaps best known as the spokesperson for Motel 6. He made his national broadcasting debut in 1984 as a commentator for National Public Radio's *All Things Considered*; he currently hosts the PBS/Travel Channel co-production *Travels on America's Historic Trails with Tom Bodett*, which has received two Emmy nominations. His voice can also be heard on Steven Spielberg's *Animaniacs, Pinky and the Brain, Saturday Night Live,* and *National Geographic Explorer*. He is the author of five books and has recorded fifteen audiocassettes.

Tom Bodett has lived in Alaska for the past twenty-three years.

Discussion Questions

- If you and a sibling were twelve and thirteen years old, would your parents leave you alone for a couple of weeks?
- Would it be exciting to live in a rural Alaskan home?
- Did the author describe the surroundings adequately?
- If you were Ivan or September, what would you have done differently?
- Did anything ever happen to you just as it happened in this book?
- If you could talk to the author, what would you ask?
- What does this story make you want to learn more about?
- Did you hope an event in the book would not happen but it happened anyway?
- Was the ending as you expected, or were there surprises?
- What was the main issue or problem that the plot revolved around?

Content Area Connections

Social Studies

Students may:

- Make a chart of the geography of Alaska, listing the tallest mountains, largest lakes, longest rivers, and so on.
- Review the history of the Klondike Gold Rush and record some statistics about it on a poster.

Science

Students may:

- Research aurora borealis and create a poster sharing their findings.
- Find out about the life of an Alaskan salmon and prepare a report for their classmates.

Language Arts

Students may:

- Dramatize a portion of the story and record it as a play for the radio.
- Write a different ending for the story.

Technology

Students may:

- Research on the Internet the Exxon Valdez accident and its impact on the Alaskan ecosystem.

Mapping

Students may:

- Create a concept map of the history of Alaska.

Snack: Ice cream sundaes

Annotated Titles About Alaska

Armstrong, Jennifer. *Spirit of Endurance.* Crown Publishing Group, Incorporated, 2000.

This picture book is the true story of Sir Ernest Henry Shackleton's voyage to the Antarctic and his failed attempt to trek from one side of Antarctica to the other. At the end of the Antarctic summer, the Endurance was stuck in the ice while in the Weddell Sea, and ten months later the crew had to abandon the ship. Then the real adventure began.

———. *Shipwreck at the Bottom of the World.* Crown Publishing Group, Incorporated, 1998.

All the men on Sir Ernest Henry Shakleton's expedition across the Antarctic survived when they lost their ship. The crew was stranded in the most hostile environment in the world and survived against enormous odds.

Brown, Tricia. *Children of the Midnight Sun: Young Native Voices of Alaska.* Alaska Northwest Books, 1998.

Alaskan culture and lifestyles are experiencing tremendous changes due to "the introduction of television, improved communications and transportation systems, and, of course, the computer and the Internet." With text and photographs, the author gives a glimpse of Alaskan children's lives and the challenges they face.

Burleigh, Robert. *Black Whiteness: Admiral Byrd Alone in the Antarctic.* Atheneum Books for Young Readers, 1998.

Based on the diary of Admiral Byrd, the author, in poetic prose, tells of Byrd's loneliness, illness, and survival when he spent almost six months alone in Antarctica.

DeVries, Douglas. *Gold Rush Runaway: A Historical Novel of Alaska Exploration and Adventure.* Jade Ram Publishing, 1997.

Fictitious Sven Olafsen, fourteen, comes in contact with Lt. Joseph Castner several times as a mule handler, stowaway, fireman, and runaway. Sven needs to get to Circle City, which is where his family last heard from his father. Lt. Castner was assigned to the Alaskan expedition to explore a route through Canada from Prince William Sound to the Yukon River via Circle City. After many encounters, Lt. Castner allows Sven to come along to help with the mules and other chores as they face the Alaskan weather and wilderness in 1898.

Dils, Tracey. *The Exxon Valdez.* Chelsea House Publishers, 2001.

The Exxon Valdez was three football fields in length and one of the largest tankers in the world. It was loaded with fifty-three million gallons of crude oil when it departed the remote village of Valdez and navigated Prince William Sound. As the result of a combination of errors discovered later, the Exxon Valdez hit Bligh Reef and tore a hole in its bottom on March 24, 1989. Eight of its thirteen cargo tanks split open, and the Exxon Valdez became the largest oil spill in United States history. This is the story of the great catastrophe, the clean-up, and the ramifications.

Flowers, Pam with Ann Dixon. *Alone Across the Arctic: One Woman's Epic Journey by Dog Team.* Graphic Arts Center Publishing Company, 2001.

Pam Flowers was the first American and first woman to travel 2,500 miles from Barrow, Alaska, to Repulse Bay, Canada. This is her story, a dream come true.

George, Jean Craighead. *Julie.* HarperTrophy, 1996.

In this continuation of the story *Julie of the Wolves*, Julie returns home to live with her father and finds to her sorrow that he has abandoned many of the Eskimo traditions. This change puts Julie's wolf friends in danger.

——. *Julie of the Wolves.* HarperCollins Juvenile Books, 1987.

Thirteen-year-old Miyax has a choice. She can remain in an arranged marriage or journey across the frozen tundra of Alaska to visit her friend Amy in San Francisco. She becomes lost and makes friends with a pack of wolves to survive.

——. *Julie's Wolf Pack.* HarperCollins Juvenile Books, 1996.

This is the third adventure of Julie and the wolves. This story is told with the wolves as the main characters and Julie on the sidelines.

——. *Water Sky.* HarperTrophy, 1989.

This book addresses the issues of conservation and cultural heritage as New Englander Lincoln Noah Stonewright spends the summer in Alaska with the family of an Eskimo whaling captain.

Hill, Kirkpatrick. *The Year of Miss Agnes.* Margaret K. McElderry, 2000.

What will the new teacher at the small Alaskan Athabascan village on the Koyukuk River be like? Will she soon leave because she doesn't like the smell of fish? Miss Agnes has been in the country a long time, and she catches the children's attention when she says she doesn't believe in grades and starts school by throwing out the old books. Miss Agnes is only going to stay the one year and then return to England—or perhaps not.

Hobbs, Will. *Jason's Gold.* HarperTrophy, 1999.

Jason was named by his father for the Greek mythological hero who sought treasure. Likewise, Jason, who left home three years after his father died, finally free from the life of a "wage slave," makes his way across the country from Seattle to New York. When he is in New York on July 17, 1897, news breaks about gold in Alaska. Jason immediately begins to ride the rails back to Seattle. He plans to take the $500 his father willed to him, plus $250 from each of his two brothers, to outfit himself. When Jason arrives at his brother's boarding house, a letter is waiting for him. Both brothers came down with a bad case of Klondike fever and left for Alaska two days earlier with all the inheritance money. Jason is determined to follow, and the adventure begins.

———. *Down the Yukon.* HarperCollins Publishers, 2001.

In this sequel to *Jason's Gold*, Jason has caught up with his brothers and they own a lumber mill in Dawson City. His brother Ethan, in a drunken stupor, signs away the ownership of the mill for a fraction of its worth. Jason vows to get the mill back and he knows just the way. He will enter the Great Race, a race from Dawson City to Nome, Alaska.

Hoyt-Goldsmith, Diane. *Arctic Hunter.* Holiday House, 1992.

This is the story of Reggie, a ten-year-old boy who lives in Kotzebue, Alaska, north of the Arctic Circle. During the summer the family goes to the same camp every year to hunt and fish for the food they will need during the upcoming year. While at camp they practice the skills that have allowed their people to survive in the harsh climate.

Ramsey, James. *Winter Watch.* Alaska Northwest Books, 1989.

The author spent nine months from September to June in a remote one-room log cabin in Northwest Alaska. The nearest Eskimo village was forty miles away. This is his diary of what happened during that time.

Shahan, Sherry. *Frozen Stiff.* Laurel-Leaf Books, 1999.

Cody does not like sneaking around and would have felt better if she had told her mother her plans. However, Aunt Jessie would never have said yes to her son Derek's and Cody's kayak and camping trip. They would be gone only two nights, paddling down the Alaskan Fjord. They planned to be back before Cody's mom and aunt returned from their shopping trip to Juneau. After their first night of camping, Cody's overturned kayak, food, and life vest were drifting in the fjord. From her limited wilderness experience, Cody knows that a trip that started badly would continue to get worse.

Shepherd, Donna Walsh. *Alaska.* Children's Book Press, 1999.

This book is one of the America the Beautiful series. Alaska is the largest state and the second least populated. The author describes the history, people, physical and economic features, climate and geographical regions, cities and towns, quick facts, and a timeline.

Williams, Jean Kinney. *Mathew Henson: Polar Adventurer.* Franklin Watts, 1994.

When Matthew Henson was fourteen, he walked forty miles to Baltimore, Maryland, signed on as a cabin boy, and sailed to Asia, Africa, and Europe. When the captain died, Matthew signed on to a fishing schooner and soon learned that people paid more attention to the color of his skin than to his abilities. Eventually he met Robert Peary and this began the relationship of explorer and assistant that lasted over twenty years. They would spend many years exploring the Arctic, and in 1909 they planted the American flag at the North Pole. Peary described his assistant Henson with the words, "I can't get along without him."

Additional Titles About Alaska

DeClements, Barthe. *The Bite of the Gold Bug: A Story of the Alaskan Gold Rush.* Penguin Putnam Books for Young Readers, 1992.

Dixon, Ann. *The Sleeping Lady.* Graphic Arts Center Publishing Company, 1994.

Dolan, Ellen M. *Susan Butcher and the Iditarod Trail.* Walker, 1992.

Huntington, Sidney. *Shadows on the Koyukuk: An Alaskan Native's Life Along the River.* Alaska Northwest Books, 1993.

Jones, Charlotte. *Yukon Gold: The Story of the Klondike Gold Rush.* Holiday House, 1998.

Kittredge, Frances. *Neeluk: An Eskimo Boy in the Days of the Whaling Ships.* Graphic Arts Center Publishing Company, 2001.

Levi, Steven C. *Cowboys of the Sky: The Story of Alaska's Bush Pilots.* Walker, 1996.

Martin, Nora. *The Eagle's Shadow.* Scholastic Incorporated, 1997.

Mikaelsen, Ben. *Touching Spirit Bear.* HarperCollins Children's Book Group, 2001.

Miller, Luree and Scott. *Alaska: Pioneer Stories of the 21st Frontier.* Penguin Putnam Books for the Young Reader, 1991.

Murphy, Claire Rudolf. *Gold Rush Women.* Graphic Arts Center Publishing Company, 1997.

——. *To the Summit.* Penguin Putnam Books for Young Readers, 1992.

Paulsen, Gary. *Dogteam.* Bantam Doubleday Dell Books for Young Readers, 1995.

Riddles, Libby. *Storm Run: The Story of the First Woman to Win the Iditarod Sled Dog Race.* Sasquatch Books, 2001.

Smith, Sherri L. *Lucy the Giant.* Delacorte Press, 2002.

Tiulana, Paul and Vivian Senungetuk. *Wise Words of Paul Tiulana: An Inupiat Alaskan's Life.* Franklin Watts, 1998.

Vanasse, Deb. *Out of the Wilderness.* Clarion Books, 1999.

Teacher Resource About Alaska

Bednar, Nancy. *Gold Rush Thematic Unit.* Teacher Created Materials, 1994.

Web Sites About Alaska

Online Materials about Alaska's Native History and Culture
http://www.alaskool.org/
Exxon Valdez Oil Spill Trustee Council
http://www.oilspill.state.ak.us/
Images from the Exxon Valdez Oil Spill
http://response.restoration.noaa.gov/photos/exxon/exxon.html
The Writing Den: The Klondike Gold Rush
http://www2.actden.com/writ_den/h08/direct.htm
Alaska for Kids
http://www.state.ak.us/kids/
Information About the State of Alaska
http://www.dced.state.ak.us/tourism/student.htm
Alaska Volcano Observatory
http://www.avo.alaska.edu/
Auroras: Paintings in the Sky
http://www.exploratorium.edu/learning_studio/auroras/

Web Sites About Tom Bodett

Tom Bodett's Home Page
http://www.bodett.com/
An Interview with Tom Bodett at Amazon.com
http://www.amazon.com/exec/obidos/show-interview/
b-t-odettom/103–0985017–1568642
America's Historic Trails—with Tom Bodett
http://www.travelsmallworld.com/america'shistorictrails.htm

Contact Publisher:

Knopf Books for Young Readers
Random House, Inc.
1540 Broadway
New York, NY 10036

11

Skeleton Man by Joseph Bruchac
(HarperCollins Children's Book Group, 2001)

Genre: Legends, Mystery
Theme: Native American Legends

Introduction

The *Skeleton Man* is a good book club to start with in the fall, preferably October or November. Play Native American music as a background during your discussion. This suspenseful novel introduces the author of numerous books on Native American legends. If there are Native Americans in your locale, have information on hand to share with your group concerning their location, customs, and other interesting facts. How have the

Native Americans in your area influenced your state in the past and in the present? Inform your group about Joseph Bruchac and how he works to preserve the culture and stories of Native Americans. Discuss if there is something they could support and help preserve.

Summary of *Skeleton Man*

Sixth grader Molly's parents mysteriously disappear one night. The local authorities are delighted when an elderly man shows up to claim Molly, stating he is her great uncle and sharing family photos. Molly knows this man is not her great uncle but she does not know how to prove it. He locks her in her room at night and allows her only to attend school in the day. Molly heeds her dreams about her Mohawk heritage, Mohawk stories she has heard, and her great uncle. She does some great detective work and solves the mystery of her parents' disappearance.

Information About Joseph Bruchac

Joseph Bruchac lives with his wife, Carol, in the Adirondack foothills town of Greenfield Center, New York, in the same house where his maternal grandparents raised him. Much of his writing has Native American themes and draws on the land he lives on as well as his Abenaki ancestry. Although his American Indian heritage is only one part of an ethnic background that includes Slovak and English blood, those native roots are the ones by which he has been most nourished. He, his younger sister, Margaret, and his two grown sons, James and Jesse, continue to work extensively in projects involving the preservation of Abenaki culture, language, and traditional native skills, including performing traditional and contemporary Abenaki music with the Dawnland Singers.

Bruchac holds a B.A. from Cornell University, an M.A. in Literature and Creative Writing from Syracuse Univesity, and a Ph.D. in Comparative Literature from the Union Institute of Ohio. His work as an educator includes eight years of directing a college program for Skidmore College inside a maximum security prison. With his wife, Carol, he is the founder and director of the Greenfield Review Literary Center and Greenfield Review Press. He has edited a number of highly praised anthologies of contemporary poetry and fiction, including *Songs from This Earth on Turtle's Back, Breaking Silence* (winner of an American Book Award), and *Returning the Gift*.

His poems, articles, and stories have appeared in over 500 publications, from *American Poetry Review, Cricket,* and *Aboriginal Voices* to *National Geographic, Parabola,* and *Smithsonian Magazine*.

Bruchac has authored more than seventy books for adults and children, including *The First Strawberries, Keepers of the Earth* (coauthored with Michael Caduto), *Tell Me a Tale, When the Chenoo Howls* (coauthored with his son, James), his autobiography *Bowman's Store,* and such novels as *Dawn Land, The Waters Between, Arrow Over the Door,* and *The Heart of a Chief.* Forthcoming titles include *Squanto's Journey* (Harcourt), a picture book; *Sacajawea's Story* (Harcourt), a historical novel; *Crazy Horse's Vision* (Lee & Low), a picture book; and *Pushing Up the Sky* (Dial), a collection of plays for children.

His honors include a Rockefeller Humanities fellowship, a National Endowment for the Arts Writing Fellowship for Poetry, the Cherokee Nation Prose Award, the Knickerbocker Award, the Hope S. Dean Award for Notable Achievement in Children's Literature, and both the 1998 Writer of the Year Award and the 1998 Storyteller of the Year Award from the Wordcraft Circle of Native Writers and Storytellers. In 1999, he received a Lifetime Achievement Award from the Native Writers Circle of the America.

As a professional teller of the traditional tales of the Adirondacks and the native peoples of the Northeastern Woodlands, Joseph Bruchac has performed widely in Europe and throughout the United States from Florida to Hawaii and has been featured at such events as the British Storytelling Festival and the National Storytelling Festival in Jonesboro, Tennessee. He has been a storyteller-in-residence for Native American organizations and schools throughout the continent, including the Institute of Alaska Native Arts and the Onondaga Nation School. He discusses native culture and his books and does storytelling programs at dozens of elementary and secondary schools each year as a visiting author.

Discussion Questions

- Do you like books about ghosts and skeletons?
- Did you suspect what happened to Molly's parents?
- How does this story compare to other Native American legends you have read?
- If you could talk to the author, what questions would you ask?
- What was the most important thing you learned from this book?
- Did this book leave you feeling that there is more to tell?
- Was the ending of the book what you expected or were there surprises?
- What was more important—the plot or the main character?
- Will you read other books by this author? Why or why not?
- After you finish the book, go back and look at the cover. Is it a good illustration for this story? Why or why not?

Content Area Connections

Language Arts

Students may:

- Read some of the legends from this Web site and then write a legend in a similar style to explain something about the world they live in. Native American Lore: http://www.ilhawaii.net/~stony/loreindx .html

- Create a commercial for the book and present it to their classmates.
- Write a news article for the local newspaper about what happened in the story.

Social Studies

Students may:

- Select a Native American tribe and find out all they can about them. Prepare a report for the class.
- Create their own Indian newspaper and learn about contemporary Native American life: http://www.indiancountry.com

Art

Students may:

- Create an Ojo de Dios (Eye of God) by using two craft sticks in the shape of a cross and winding different colored yarns around the stick. Do some research to find out why the Native Americans made these and how they looked.

Technology

Students may:

- Research the author, Joseph Bruchac, on the Internet. Prepare a presentation about his life and his efforts with Native Americans.

Mapping

Students may:

- Create a map of the major tribes in the United States today. Identify their locations and give a brief description.

Snack: Cornbread, pumpkin pie, nuts

Annotated Titles About Native American Legends

Berman, Karen. *American Indian Traditions and Ceremonies.* JG Books, 1997.
Native Americans showed respect, gave thanks, and prayed for good luck by participating in many ceremonies. Their lives were based around tribal traditions and ceremonies. This book is divided into the following chapters: cycle of life, sustenance, daily life, war and peace, and tribal society.

Bierhorst, John. *The Naked Bear: Folktales of the Iroquois.* William Morrow and Company, 1987.
The six nations of the Iroquois were noted for their master storytellers. Included in this book are sixteen of their best stories with the figures of speech the master storyteller would have used.

Ciment, James, PhD. *Scholastic Encyclopedia of the North American Indian.* Scholastic Reference, 1996.
One hundred forty-three groups of Native Americans are arranged in alphabetical order with highlighted text boxes. Several interesting maps and places to see in the various geographical regions are included at the end.

Cooney, Caroline B. *The Ransom of Mercy Carter.* Delacorte Press, 2001.
In 1704 Mohawks attacked the settlement of Deerfield, Massachusetts, and captured Mercy Carter and over 100 other settlers. They were taken on a grueling trip of 300 miles to Canada to be ransomed, sold, or adopted by French or Indian families. Mercy is adopted by her abductor and becomes an Indian daughter. When a ransom is finally offered for her return, she is torn between the two cultures and doesn't know if she will accept it.

Hotze, Sollace. *A Circle Unbroken.* Clarion Books, 1988.
Kata Wi, seventeen, senses that the white men who are furtively coming on horseback are coming for her. Seven years ago she was captured by a band of renegade Sioux, raped, and finally adopted by a loving Sioux chief and his wife. The men return Kata Wi—or Rachel Porter, as she was known—to her minister father. Her father will not tolerate anything that reminds him that the Indians caused him to lose two children and his wife in the raid. After a year of trying to adjust to the white man's society, Rachel asks to return to her Indian life. She knows that otherwise she will die. How will her father bear to let Rachel go again after just finding her?

Lelooska, Chief. *Echoes of the Elders: The Stories and Paintings of Chief Lelooska.* DK Publishing, Inc., 1997.
The elders entrusted the old stories to Chief Lelooska. Prior to his death, he put together five traditional stories with accompanying paintings that show respect and reverence for all of nature. A CD is included that has background music accompanying his retelling of tales.

Native Americans. Time Life Books, 1995.
The chapters are as follows: The People, On the Move, Making a Living, Homes, Ceremonies and Ritual, and A Changing World. The text is very readable and accompanied by numerous illustrations.

Norman, Howard. *How Glooskap Outwits the Ice Giants: And Other Tales of the Maritime Indians.* Little, Brown, 1989.
A Glooskap is considered the first human being according to legend in the Northeast region. The Glooskap would roam between the Maritime Provinces and Maine. These six stories relate how the Glooskap created the Indian People and protected them from evil.

Paulson, Gary. *Canyons.* Laurel-Leaf Books, 1991.
Coyote Runs's first raid will prove his manhood—if he survives. More than 100 years later, fifteen-year-old Brennan finds a skull on a canyon ledge. He learns that it is the skull of an Apache boy killed by soldiers in 1864. Brennan becomes obsessed with returning the skull to the appropriate burial ground so Coyote Runs can find peace.

Philip, Neil, ed. *In a Sacred Manner I Live: Native American Wisdom.* Clarion Books, 1997.
"To live in a sacred manner is to live with respect for the environment, for the community, and for oneself." Listen to speakers and writers of the 1600s up to contemporary time.

Wood, Marion. *Spirits, Heroes, and Hunters from North American Indian Mythology.* Peter Bedrick Books, 1981.
A collection of myths and legends as varied as the tribes they represent.

Additional Titles About Native American Legends

Bierhorst, John, ed. *The White Deer and Other Stories Told by the Lenape.* Morrow Avon, 1995.

Caduto, Michael J. and Joseph Bruchac. *Keepers of the Night: Native American Stories and Nocturnal Activities for Children.* Fulcrum Publishing, 1994.

Curry, Jane Louise. *Back in the Beforetime.* Aladdin Paperbacks, 2001.

Dalal, Anita. *Myths of the Native Americans.* Raintree Steck-Vaughn Publishers, 2001.

———. *Myths of Pre-Columbian America.* Raintree Steck-Vaughn Publishers, 2001.

Houston, James R. *The Falcon Bow: An Arctic Legend.* Penguin Putnam Books for Young Readers, 1992.

Jameson, W.C. *Buried Treasures of the Appalachians: Legends of Homestead Caches, Indian Mines, and Loot from Civil War Raids.* August House Publishers, Inc., 1991.

Keeper, Berry. *The Old Ones Told Me: American Indian Stories for Children.* Binford & Mort Publishing, 2000.

Lacapa, Michael. *Antelope Woman: An Apache Folktale.* Northland Publishing, 1992.

Luenn, Nancy. *The Miser on the Mountain: A Nisqually Legend of Mount Rainier.* Sasquatch Books, 1997.

Max, Jill. *Spider Spins a Story: Fourteen Legends from Native America.* Northland Publishing, 1997.

Mayfield, Thomas. *Adopted by Indians: A True Story.* Heyday Books, 1997.

Mayo, Gretchen W. *Meet Tricky Coyote.* Walker, 1993.

Moon, Grace Purdie. *Indian Legends in Rhyme.* Kiva Publishing, Inc., 2000.

Olson, Dennis L. *Warrior Wisdom: Native American Animal Legends.* Creative Publishing International Inc., 1999.

Priest, George E. *The Great Winged Monster of the Piasa Valley: The Legend of the Piasa.* Alton Museum of History and Art, Inc., 1998.

Seymour, Tryntje V.N. *The Gift of Changing Woman.* Henry Holt Books for the Young Reader, 1993.

Shenandoah, Joanne. *Skywoman: Legends of the Iroquois.* Clear Light Publishers, 1997.

Steptoe, John. *The Story of Jumping Mouse: A Native American Legend.* Turtle-back Books, 1984.

Taylor, C.J. *Bones in the Basket: Native Stories of the Origin of People.* Tundra Books of Northern New York, 1994.

———. *The Secret of the White Buffalo: An Oglala Sioux Legend.* Tundra Books of Northern New York, 1993.

Wood, Marion. *Myths and Civilizations of the Native Americans.* McGraw-Hill Children's Publishing, 2000.

Annotated Titles by Joseph Bruchac

The Boy Who Lived with the Bears: And Other Iroquois Stories. HarperCollins Publishers, 1995.

Bruchac, a storyteller with a good mind, retells six Iroquois tales that "teach important lessons about caring and responsibility and the dangers of selfishness and pride."

The First Strawberries: A Cherokee Story. Dial Books for Young Readers, 1993.
This is a creation story of how the first strawberries came to be.

Four Ancestors: Stories, Songs, and Poems from Native North America. Bridge-Water Books, 1996.

Some say fire, earth, water, and air are components of the Human Being. Therefore it might be stated that they are our ancestors. This book is divided into the four elements of creation and celebrated through the stories, songs, poems, and prayers of Native North Americans.

The Great Ball Game: A Muskogee Story. Dial Books for Young Readers, 1994.

The birds and the animals had an argument regarding who was better. They decided to play a ballgame to determine who was best. The bat did not know whose side to play on. The bear invited the bat to play on the animals' team, and with the help of the bat, the animals won. The punishment for the birds was to fly south for half of each year.

The Journal of Jesse Smoke: A Cherokee Boy, Trail of Tears, 1838 (My Name Is America). Scholastic Incorporated, 2001.

The Cherokee nation has been reduced to a small portion of where the present states of Georgia, Tennessee, and North Carolina come together. Now the United States government wants to move these hardworking and industrious people west of the Mississippi. This is Jesse Smoke's diary of events leading up to and during the forced removal of the Cherokees to Oklahoma, or the Trail of Tears.

Lasting Echoes: An Oral History of Native American People. Silver Whistle, 1997.

This history of Native Americans is told from their perspective with excerpts from songs, traditional stories, poetry, myths, personal experiences, legends, dreams, and visions.

With Gayle Ross. *The Story of the Milky Way: A Cherokee Tale.* Dial Books for Young Readers, 1995.

This is the story of how the people came together and frightened the spirit dog up into the sky. When they did so, cornmeal spilled from the dog's mouth and thus the Milky Way was formed.

Additional Titles by Joseph Bruchac

The Arrow over the Door. Dial Books for Young Readers, 1998.

Between Earth and Sky: Legends of Native American Sacred Places. Harcourt, 1999.

Bowman's Store: A Journey to Myself. Lee & Low, 2001.

A Boy Called Slow: The True Story of Sitting Bull. Philomel Books, 1995.

Children of the Longhouse. Puffin Books, 1998.

The Circle of Thanks. BridgeWater Books, 1996.

Dog People: Native Dog Stories. Fulcrum Publishing, 1995.

Eagle Song. Dial Books for Young Readers, 1997.

The Earth Under Sky Bear's Feet: Native American Poems of the Land. Penguin Putnam Books for Young Readers, 1995.

Flying with the Eagle, Racing the Great Bear: Stories from Native North America. Troll Associates, 1993.

The Girl Who Married the Moon: Tales from Native North America. Troll Communications, 1994.

The Heart of a Chief: A Novel. Dial Books for Young Readers, 1998.

How Chipmunk Got His Stripes: A Tale of Bragging and Teasing. Dial Books for Young Readers, 2001.

Keepers of the Animals: Native American Stories and Wildlife Activities for Children. Fulcrum Publishing, 1997.

Keepers of the Earth: Native American Stories and Environmental Activities for Children. Fulcrum Publishing, 1997.

Keepers of Life: Discovering Plants through Native American Stories and Earth Activities for Children. Fulcrum Publishing, 1997.

Keepers of the Night: Native American Stories and Nocturnal Activities for Children. Fulcrum Publishing, 1994.

Native American Animal Stories. Fulcrum Publishing, 1992.

Native American Games and Stories. Fulcrum Publishing, 2000.

Native American Gardening: Stories, Projects and Recipes for Families. Fulcrum Publishing, 1996.

Native American Stories. Fulcrum Publishing, 1991.

The Native American Sweat Lodge: History and Legends. The Crossing Press, 1993.

Native Plant Stories. Fulcrum Publishing, 1995.

No Borders. Holy Cow! Press, 1999.

Return of the Sun: Native American Tales from the Northeast Woodland. The Crossing Press, 1990.

Sacajawea: The Story of Bird Woman and the Lewis and Clark Expedition. Silver Whistle, 2000.

Tell Me a Tale: A Book About Storytelling. Harcourt, 1997.

Thirteen Moons on Turtle's Back: A Native American Year of Moons. Philomel Books, 1992.

Translators' Son. Cross Cultural Press, 1994.

Turtle Meat and Other Stories. Holy Cow! Press, 1992.

The Waters Between: A Novel of the Dawn Land. University Press of New England, 1998.

When the Chenoo Howls: Native American Tales of Terror. Walker, 1999.

Teacher Resources About Native American Legends

Caduto, Michael J. and Joseph Bruchac. *Keepers of the Animals: Native American Stories and Wildlife Activities for Children.* Fulcrum Publishing, 1997.

Caduto, Michael J. and Joseph Bruchac. *Keepers of the Earth: Native American Stories and Environmental Activities for Children.* Fulcrum Publishing, 1999.

Caduto, Michael J. and Joseph Bruchac. *Keepers of Life: Discovering Plants through Native American Stories and Wildlife Activities for Children.* Fulcrum Publishing, 1997.

Caduto, Michael J. and Joseph Bruchac. *Keepers of the Night: Native American Stories and Nocturnal Activities for Children.* Fulcrum Publishing, 1994.

Hoven, Leigh. *Native American Thematic Unit.* Teacher Created Materials, 1990.

Kronowitz, Ellen and Barbara Wally. *Native American Arts and Cultures.* Teacher Created Materials, 2000.

Major-Tingey, Susan. *Native American Art Projects.* Scholastic Professional Books, 1995.

Robbins, Mari Lu. *Native Americans.* Teacher Created Materials, 1994.

Zaun, Kathy. *Native American Whole Language Thematic Unit.* Instructional Fair, 1994.

Web Sites About Native American Legends

Native American Poems and Stories
http://nativetech.org/poetry/
Marilee's Native American Links
http://www.ameritech.net/users/macler/nativeamericans.html
Native Americans
http://www.westnyacklib.org/NatAmer.htm
Native Child
http://www.nativechild.com/
Native American Shelters
http://www.anthro.mankato.msus.edu/prehistory/settlements/index.shtml

Southwest Native Americans
http://inkido.indiana.edu/w310work/romac/swest.htm
South Dakota—Great Sioux Nation
http://www.travelsd.com/history/sioux/
Native American Internet Resources
http://falcon.jmu.edu/ ~ ramseyil/native.htm
The Nation's Leading American News Source: Indian Country-Today
http://www.indiancountry.com

Web Sites About Joseph Bruchac

Joseph Bruchac: Storyteller and Writer
http://www.josephbruchac.com/
A Chat with Joseph Bruchac
http://www.wordsmith.org/chat/bruchac.html
An Interview with Joseph Bruchac
http://www.education.wisc.edu/ccbc/bruchac.htm
Meet the Author: Joseph Bruchac
http://www.eduplace.com/kids/hmr/mtai/bruchac.html
Meet the Authors and Illustrators: Joseph Bruchac
http://www.childrenslit.com/f_bruchac.html
Meet Celebrity Author Joseph Bruchac
http://www.scottforesman.com/families/authors/bruchac.html
Booktalk: Joseph Bruchac
http://www.leeandlow.com/booktalk/bruchac.html
Joseph Bruchac on Native American Literature
http://abaa.org/collectors/bc-bruchac.html
Joseph Bruchac: Interview with the Author
http://www.nea.org/readacross/multi/jbruchac.html
Joseph Bruchac
http://www.unomaha.edu/ ~ unochlit/bruchac.html
Author—Joseph Bruchac
http://www.harperchildrens.com/catalog/author_xml.asp?
authorID = 1244
The Ndakinna Wilderness Project
http://www.ndakinna.com/

Contact Publisher:

HarperCollins Children's Books
1350 Avenue of the Americas
New York, NY 10019

Joseph Bruchac
P.O. Box 308
Greenfield Center, NY 12833

12

Ties That Bind, Ties That Break by
Lensey Namioka (Delacorte Press, 1999)

Genre: Multicultural
Theme: China

Introduction

Lensey Namioka writes about China and Japan so both cultures can be explored. Introduce this session with a booktalk on *Shipwrecked: The True Adventure of a Japanese Boy* or ask a local emigrant to come and speak to your group about what it is like to leave your birthplace and begin a new life in another country. Discuss the title: what are some of the ties that bind you to your home and country and what are some of the ties that could break you? The featured book will inspire discussion on the Chinese custom of foot binding, customs around the world, the countries of China and Japan, emigration, arranged marriages, and the role of women in history and present day. Decorate the room with a Chinese theme and play Asian music in the background.

Summary of *Ties That Bind, Ties That Break*

Ailin is fighting a quiet war against Chinese tradition. She is the Third Sister in the Tao family and has watched her two older sisters go through the painful process of having their feet bound. In China in 1911, all the women of good families followed this ancient tradition. But Ailin loves to run away from her governess and play games with her male cousins. Knowing she will never run again if her feet are bound, Ailin rebels and refuses to follow this torturous tradition. Her father agrees and feels that the old customs will fade.

As a result, however, the family of her intended husband breaks their marriage agreement. And as she enters adolescence, Ailin finds that her family is no longer willing to support her. Chinese society leaves few options for a single woman of good family, but Ailin, with a bold conviction and an indomitable spirit, is determined to forge her own destiny. Her story is a tribute to all women whose courage created new options for the generations who came after them. A note on the Chinese tradition of foot binding is included.

Information About Lensey Namioka

Lensey Namioka is the author of *Yang the Youngest and His Terrible Ear* and *Yang the Third and Her Impossible Family.* Lensey Namioka was born in China and moved to the United States when she was nine. She is the only person in the world with the name Lensey; her father made it up. Her husband is Japanese, and that's why she has a Japanese last name. She is interested in both Japan and China, so she has written books about both places.

Lensey attended Radcliffe College and the University of California, Berkeley, where she majored in mathematics. She decided she liked being a writer better than being a mathematician. She has been writing for thirty years, and her books have received several recognitions. Like the Yang family, she lives in Seattle, Washington.

Discussion Questions

- How did Ailin show great courage in this story?
- How were females treated in China at the time of the story?
- Describe Ailin's relationship with her father.
- In what ways does Ailin rebel against Chinese customs?
- If Ailin returned to China at the end of the story, how do you think she would be treated by her family?
- Why is the custom of foot binding so important to this story?
- Did the author provide enough description so you could understand the way things were in China at this time?
- Have you read any other books like this one?
- Would the story have been different if Ailin were a weaker character?
- Would you recommend this story to a friend? Why or why not?

Content Area Connections

Art

Students may:

- Use a calligraphy brush and black paint/ink, try to copy some Chinese characters.

Social Studies

Students may:

- Research Chinese food and Chinese restaurants. Create a poster of their special dishes.
- Describe chopsticks and write step-by-step instructions for using them.
- Research who immigrated to America in the past and who is immigrating today.

Science

Students may:

- Research tuberculosis. Ailin's father died of tuberculosis in the story. Is it a threat today?
- Research silkworms. What has synthetic silk done to the silkworm industry?

Technology

Students may:

- Research foot binding on the Internet. Is it still practiced? What are the physical problems women experienced as a result of foot binding?

Mapping

Students may:

- Create a concept map. Put the word China in the center and add subcategories of Land/Geography, People, and Social Customs. Brainstorm existing knowledge. Add to the map as they learn more about China.

Snack: Fortune cookies, Chinese noodles, tea

Annotated Titles About China

Blumberg, Rhonda. *Shipwrecked! The True Adventures of a Japanese Boy.* HarperCollins Publishers, 2001.

In 1830 Japan was an isolated country. Anyone who left Japan was not allowed to return. Anyone who did return would most likely be killed. The seaports were closed to foreign vessels and visitors until 1853 when Commodore Matthew Perry anchored in Edo Bay and refused to leave. This is the story of Manjiro, a lowly fisherman who was blown out to sea in a storm. He was rescued by a whaling ship and was the first person of Japanese descent to arrive in North America. He risked returning home and was elevated to the status of a Samurai, argued against isolationism, and "helped bring Japan into the modern world."

Compestine, Ying Chang. *The Story of Chopsticks.* Holiday House, 2001.

It was customary for Chinese people to eat with their hands. They had to wait for the food to cool, and Kuai, the youngest in his family, was always hungry because his brothers ate most of the food. Kuai discovers he doesn't have to wait for the food to cool when he uses sticks to eat. The other family members soon find their own sticks. When they are invited to a wedding, Kuai's family creates quite a commotion when they use their sticks to eat. Use this picture book to introduce chopsticks or "quick ones." Have students create their own picture book to explain how chopsticks were first invented.

Crew, Linda. *Children of the River.* Delacorte Press. 1999.

Sundara's parents shelter her from the war and spirit her away from Phnom Penh to her aunt and uncle's fishing village. Two weeks later, Sundara, age thirteen, flees Cambodia with her aunt, uncle, grandmother, and cousins to escape the Khmer Rouge army.

Three weeks at sea and the responsibility for a small baby leave Sundara struggling with guilt. She cannot go home to her land and people. Four years later, she must adjust to her new life in Oregon. Jonathan, the star football player, begins to interview Sundara for an international project. Sundara knows she should follow Cambodian customs and not ever talk to a boy. After many hardships and sorrows, Sundara finds peace with her aunt and uncle and hopes she will be reunited with her younger sister and Jonathan, her love.

Demi. *Chingis Khan.* Henry Holt and Company, 1991.

The author has based his story of the great leader Ghingis Khan on history and legend. Ghingis was a stern and fierce leader who united the Mongolian tribes and conquered China, Persia, and Russia.

Dramer, Kim. *People's Republic of China.* Children's Book Press, 1999.

This book is part of the Enchantment of the World second series. China has the largest population of any nation, and Chinese people call their country the Middle Kingdom. The author describes this land of contrasts: the environment, animals, people, history, religion, present day, and challenges.

Hoobler, Dorothy and Thomas. *The Chinese American Family Album.* Oxford University Press, 1994.

A history of Chinese immigration to America told with excerpts from family letters, diaries, official documents, newspaper articles, and literature both past and present.

Jiang, Ji-li. *Red Scarf Girl: A Memoir of the Cultural Revolution.* HarperTrophy, 1997.

Ji-li is twelve years old, and Chairman Mao has started the Cultural Revolution. It is 1966 and time to end the evil influences of old ideas, old culture, old customs, and old habits. Ji-li doesn't understand why her mom and dad do not share her enthusiasm for the new campaign. What will the future bring to Ji-li and her family?

Jimenez, Francisco. *Circuits: Stories from the Life of a Migrant Child.* University of New Mexico Press, 1997.

Short stories tell the life of a migrant child and his family, filled with hope, sorrow, hardships, anger, and love. The author was second of seven brothers and sisters. At a very early age he was responsible for the care of his younger siblings while his parents and older brother worked in the fields picking cotton, strawberries, or grapes in California. He went to school when he could be spared from the fields. The family moved to where work was available and lived in tents, garages, or barracks. When Francisco was in fifth grade, he was invited to a school friend's house. It was the first time he had been inside a house. The stories of this award-winning book give one a glimpse of the struggle and hardships of the American Dream.

Mah, Adeline Yen. *The Chinese Cinderella.* Delacorte Press, 1999.

This is the true story of the first fourteen years of Wu Mei (later named Adeline when her father remarries), who grew up in Shanghai and Hong Kong. Wu Mei is the fifth child and considered bad luck by her family because her mother died in childbirth. Her father remarries and has two additional children. Life becomes unfair and difficult for the elder children. In one episode the stepmother is beating the youngest child, and Wu Mei (Adeline) intervenes. The stepmother states she will never forgive her arrogance and that she will pay so she'd better watch out. The only way Wu Mei receives any recognition and acceptance is through her studies and writing. They will be her salvation.

Mann, Elizabeth. *The Great Wall.* Mikaya Press, 1997.

The Great Wall was built to keep China safe from Mongol warriors. The wall took 200 years to build and was thirty feet high and shaped to fit the terrain. This is the story of this massive defense system and the downfall of the Ming dynasty.

Na, An. *A Step from Heaven.* Front Street, 2001.

Young Ju was four years old and was going to America. She thought America was another name for heaven. When she arrived with her mother and father, she learned from her aunt that it was not exactly heaven but one step from heaven. Unfortunately, many of their problems were not solved by moving to the United States. Young Ju's brother, Joon, was born shortly after they arrived and was immediately her father's favorite. Her mother (Uhmma) and father (Apa) work many jobs to get ahead, and it is Young Ju's job to do well in school so she will have all the advantages America offers. Apa returns to his old ways of alcohol and violence. No one is spared—not Uhmma, Joon, or Young Ju. One night when Young Ju returns from a visit with her forbidden friend Amanda, Apa is unexpectedly home and questions Young Ju about where she has been. When she replies that she was at the library, he knows she is lying and that will not be tolerated. The violence and abuse begins and carries over against her mother. Young Ju makes a decision to call 911 and their lives change once again.

Rumford, James. *Traveling Man: The Journey of Ibn Battuta 1325–1354.* Houghton Mifflin Company, 2001.

With brief text and illustrations and illuminations, the author tells about the journey and adventures of Ibn Battuta. Ibn left Morocco when he was twenty-one, and 75,000 miles later he had traveled to Egypt, India, China, and Russia. "Traveling—it offers you a hundred roads to adventure, and gives your heart wings!"

Sis, Peter. *Tibet through the Red Box.* Farrar Straus Giroux, 1998.

This Caldecott Honor book is the story of Peter's father's trip to China and Tibet to film the construction of a highway into the Himalayas. His father kept a journal with illustrations of his experiences and kept it in a red box. As an adult, Peter is summoned home and presented with the red box that will help explain to Peter why his father is the way he is.

Williams, Brian. *Ancient China.* Viking Press, 1996.

Long before Western Civilization, the Chinese invented papermaking, printing, gun powder, and the first mechanical clock. See-through cutaways enhance the description of a Shang King's burial ground, a nobleman's house, canal boats passing through a lock, and an outer gate to the forbidden city.

Yep, Laurence. *Dragon's Gate.* HarperCollins Publishers, 1993.

Otter is forced to leave China when he accidentally kills a Manchu soldier. He flees to the Golden Mountain to follow his father and uncle, who are laborers on the transcontinental railroad.

——. *Spring Pearl: The Last Flower.* Pleasant Company Publications, 2002.

Spring Pearl's scholarly parents died when she was twelve. Her artisan father and mother taught Pearl how to read and write—unusual skills for a girl in the 1850s. Upon their death Pearl goes to live with Master Sung, a merchant and his family. When Pearl enters the house, she feels as though she is entering a prison. Pearl, with her ingenious ways, saves the Sung family and becomes one of them during the tumultuous Opium War in Canton, China.

Yin. *Coolies.* Philomel Books, 2001.

During the mid 1880s many Chinese people fled to the United States—the Golden Mountain—to escape hunger and poverty. They were hired as "coolies" (lowly workers) by the Central Pacific Railroad Company to head east, building the transcontinental railroad. Irish workers were hired by the Union Pacific Railroad Company, and they headed west until the two groups met each other at Promontory Summit, Utah. This picture book tells the story of two Chinese brothers who worked hard and suffered many hardships and prejudices until the railroad was finished and they settled in San Francisco.

Zhensun, Zheng. *A Young Painter: The Life and Paintings of Wang Yani—China's Extraordinary Young Artist.* Scholastic Incorporated, 1991.

This is the story of a young girl who has been called the Picasso of China. She had her first exhibit at the age of four. When she was fourteen, Yani traveled to Washington, D.C., for the opening of an exhibition of her work. Photographs of Yani and reproductions of her artwork are interspersed throughout.

Additional Titles About China

Alexander, Lloyd. *The Remarkable Journey of Prince Jen.* Dutton Children's Books, 1991.

Baldwin, Robert F. *Daily Life in Ancient and Modern Beijing.* Lerner Publishing Group, 1999.

Bosse, Malcolm J. *The Examination.* Farrar Straus Giroux, 1994.

Chen, Da. *China's Son: Growing Up in the Cultural Revolution.* Bantam Doubleday Dell Books for Young Readers, 2001.

Cheng, Sonia. *Myths and Civilizations of the Ancient Chinese.* McGraw-Hill Children's Publishing, 2002.

Cotterell, Arthur. *Ancient China.* Alfred A. Knopf, 1994.

Czernecki, Stefan. *Paper Lanterns.* Charlesbridge Publishing, 2000.

Fisher, Leonard Everett. *The Great Wall of China.* Aladdin Paperbacks, 1995.

Fritz, Jean. *China's Long March: 6,000 Miles of Danger.* Penguin Putnam, Incorporated, 1988.

———. *Homesick: My Own Story.* Penguin Putnam, Incorporated,1982.

Green, Robert. *China.* Lucent Books, 1999.

Hoobler, Dorothy and Thomas. *Chinese Portraits.* Raintree Steck-Vaughn Publishers, 1992.

Kent, Deborah. *Beijing.* Children's Book Press, 1996.

Lasky, Kathryn. *Lady of Ch'iao Kuo: Warrior of the South, China 531 A.D.* Scholastic Incorporated, 2001.

MacDonald, Fiona. *Marco Polo: A Journey through China.* Franklin Watts, 1998.

Mayor, John S. *The Silk Route: 7,000 Miles of History.* HarperCollins Publishers, 1995.

McLean, Virginia. *Chasing the Moon to China.* Redbird Press, Inc., 1997.

Pietrusza, David. *The Chinese Cultural Revolution.* Gale Group, 1997.

Russell, Ching R. *Child Bride.* Boyds Mills Press, 2001.

Shepard, Aaron. *The Magic Brocade: A Tale of China.* Pan Asian Publications, 2000.

Simpson, Judith. *Ancient China.* Time-Life, Inc., 1999.

Stefoff, Rebecca. *Marco Polo and the Medieval Explorers.* Chelsea House Publishers, 1992.

———. *Mao Zedong: Founder of the People's Republic of China.* Millbrook Press, Inc., 1996.

Stepanchuk, Carol. *Red Eggs and Dragon Boats: Celebrating Chinese Festivals.* Pacific View Press, 1994.

Stewart,Whitney. *Deng Xiaoping: Leader in the Changing China.* Lerner Publishing Group, 2001.

Williams, Suzanne. *Made in China: Ideas and Inventions from Ancient China.* Pacific View Press, 1996.

Yep, Laurence. *The Journal of Wong Ming-Chung: A Chinese Miner.* Scholastic Incorporated, 2000.

——. *The Cook's Family.* Penguin Putnam, Incorporated, 1998.

——. *The Rainbow People.* Harper & Row, 1989.

Zhang, Song Nan. *Cowboy on the Steppes.* Tundra Books of Northern New York, 1997.

——. *A Little Tiger in the Chinese Night: An Autobiography in Art.* Tundra Books of Northern New York, 1993.

Annotated Titles by Lensey Namioka

April and the Dragon Lady. Harcourt Brace, 1994.

April Chen, a Chinese American teenager, lives in Seattle with her widowed father, her brother, and her grandmother, The Dragon Lady. April is fitting in to American culture—she has an American boyfriend and is planning to attend college. Her plans are drastically changed when her grandmother becomes ill and she is designated to take care of her.

Den of the White Fox. Harcourt Brace and Company, 1997.

In sixteenth-century feudal Japan, wandering Samurai Matsuzo and his mentor Zenta are searching for work as mercenaries. They come upon a village with a legend about a white fox, and the twosome become involve in the village's mystery. Is the white fox a man with a mask or a menacing spirit?

An Ocean Apart, A World Away: A Novel. Delacorte Press, 2002.

In the early 1900s, in Nanjing, China, Yanyan gets the opportunity to go to America to attend Cornell University and pursue her dream of becoming a doctor. Yanyan is excited but soon finds American ways overwhelming. Just when she is beginning to feel at home and beginning to enjoy her independence, her old boyfriend arrives from China with marriage on his mind.

Yang the Eldest and His Odd Jobs. Little, Brown, 2000.

Eldest brother is the most gifted musician of the four Yang children. When his violin develops a buzz, he realizes he must buy a new violin. Eldest brother will have to get a job so he can earn some money, but what can he do? This is the last installment of four books about the Yang family.

Yang the Second and Her Secret Admirers. Little, Brown, 1998.

This is the third installment about the Yang family, who are recent immigrants to Seattle from Shanghai. The story focuses on second sister, fifteen-year-old Yinglan, who misses China and her friends and clings to Chinese customs. Her younger brother and sister scheme to get her to accept American ways.

Yang the Third and Her Impossible Family. Little, Brown, 1995.

This is the sequel to *Yang the Youngest and His Terrible Ear,* and in this story third sister Mary tries very hard to become completely Americanized while her family is holding strictly to Chinese customs and culture.

Yang the Youngest and His Terrible Ear. Dell Yearling, 1992.

In the Yang family all are musicians except fourth brother, Yang the youngest. Yang knows he cannot play in the upcoming recital without sounding awful. How can he save the recital and tell his family he likes something better than music?

Teacher Resources About China and Emigration

Granat, Diana and Stanlee Brimberg. *China.* Scholastic, 2000.

Kearns, Marsha. *Ancient China Thematic Unit.* Teacher Created Materials, 1999.

O'Connor, Jane. *Emperor's Silent Army: Terracotta Warriors.* Viking Children's Books, 2002.

Steele, Philip. *Journey Through China.* Troll Associates, 1991.

Sylvester, Diane. *Discovering China (Under the Five Themes of Geography).* Frank Schaffer Publications, 1996.

Wenli, Zhang. *The Qin Terracotta Army: Treasures of Lintong.* Scala Books, 1996.

Web Sites About China

Walk the Great Wall
http://www.walkthewall.com
Chinese Foot Binding
http://library.thinkquest.org/J0111742/footbinding.htm
Chinese Foot Binding
http://www.kidzworld.com/site/p2142.htm
Golden Legacy Curriculum: Bound Feet
http://askeric.org/cgi-in/printlessons.cgi/Virtual/Lessons/Social_Studies/Anthropology/ANT0201.html
Chinese Brush Writing
http://wwli.com/languages/zhongwen/lesson01/writing.html
Your Name in Chinese
http://www.mandarintools.com/chinesename.html
Chinese Inventions
http://www.crystalinks.com/chinainventions.html
Ancient China Crossword Puzzle
http://www.kidcrosswords.com/puzzles/html/ph44.htm

Web Sites About Lensey Namioka

Lensey Namioka's Web Site
http://www.lensey.com/index.html
Meet Celebrity Author: Lensey Namioka
http://www.scottforesman.com/families/authors/namioka.html
Meet the Author: Lensey Namioka
http://www.eduplace.com/kids/hmr/mtai/namioka.html

Contact Publisher:

Random House Children's Books
1540 Broadway
New York, NY 10036
http://www.randomhouse.com/teachers

13

Because of Winn-Dixie by Kate DiCamillo (Candlewick Press, 2000)

Genre: Animal Stories
Theme: Dogs and Pets

Introduction

Looking for a good book for your first book club? *Because of Winn-Dixie* is a charming, emotional story most students will love. This is the author's first book and it is her love of the South that helped inspire her. What is it about Opal Buloni and her dog Winn-Dixie that make this book so believable and touching? Discuss and explore the types of pets people have and why they have them. Ask the members how they protect their pets and what is being done in their area about unwanted pets? What is the most unusual pet story they have ever heard?

Summary of *Because of Winn-Dixie*

Opal moved with her father, a preacher, to Naomi, Florida. Opal was responsible for shopping at the local grocery store. At first she didn't see the dog, but when he created a friendly commotion, Opal claimed the dog was hers after the manager threatened to call the dog pound. When asked what the dog's name was, she responded "Winn-Dixie," which was the grocery store they were in. Winn-Dixie was a mutt who liked to smile using all of his teeth and had a pathological fear of thunderstorms. Winn-Dixie and Opal are responsible for soothing many lonely hearts.

Information About Kate DiCamillo

It's the pipe dream of many an aspiring author: publish your debut novel, claim a spot on the *New York Times* bestseller list, and rack up an astonishing array of awards, including a Newbery Honor, the Oscar of children's books. For Kate DiCamillo, author of the runaway charmer *Because of Winn-Dixie,* it was a dream come true—and nobody could have been more surprised than she was. "After the Newbery committee called me, I spent the whole day walking into walls. Literally," she says. "I was stunned. And very, very happy."

Kate DiCamillo was born in Philadelphia, Pennsylvania, but her family moved to Florida when she was five years old on the advice of a doctor who suggested that a warmer climate would help soothe her chronic pneumonia. "People talked more slowly and said words I had never heard before, like 'ain't' and 'y'all' and 'ma'am,'" she recalls of her first impressions. "The town was small, and everybody knew everybody else. Even if they didn't, they acted like they did. It was all so different from what I had known before, and I fell swiftly and madly in love."

Indeed, it was homesickness for Florida's warmth that helped inspire *Because of Winn-Dixie,* which Kate DiCamillo describes as "a hymn of praise to dogs, friendship, and the South." The author was experiencing one of the worst winters in Minnesota, where she had moved when she was in her twenties. "I was missing the sound of Southern people talking," she says. "And I was missing having a dog. One night before I went to sleep, I heard this little girl's voice with a Southern accent say, 'I have a dog named Winn-Dixie.' I just started writing down what India Opal Buloni was telling me."

Kate DiCamillo's second novel, *The Tiger Rising,* is "considerably darker" than *Because of Winn-Dixie,* she says, "but there's light and redemption in it." As in *Because of Winn-Dixie,* the story began with the appearance of a single character. "Rob Horton showed up in a short story I wrote and then hung around the house driving me crazy," she says. "I finally asked him what he wanted, and he told me he knew where there was a tiger." Like Opal in *Because of Winn-Dixie,* Rob struggles with the loss of a parent—a theme the author admits might be connected to her own father's leaving her family when she was five years old—and ultimately discovers the healing power of friendship. "I don't think adults always realize how much friends mean to kids," Kate DiCamillo says. "My friends have been the saving grace in my life."

Until recently Kate DiCamillo faithfully set her alarm clock for 4:00 A.M. to put in some writing time before heading off to work at a store selling used children's books. Although she now is able to devote her time to writing—and so can wake at a more reasonable hour—her regimen remains as disciplined as ever: two pages a day, five days a week.

Discussion Questions

- Why do India and her father move to Naomi, Florida?
- What is it about Winn-Dixie that makes him so appealing to Opal?
- Describe five things Opal's father has told her about her mother.
- Gloria Dump says you can't judge people by the things they did in the past. Do you agree or disagree? Why?
- Describe your favorite character in this story and include the traits this character has that you like.
- Why do you think the author chose this title?
- What do you think the relationship between Opal and her father will be in the future?
- Was the author able to involve you emotionally in this story?
- Did you feel as though you were part of the story or as though you were an observer?
- Was the ending of the story what you expected, or were you surprised?

Content Area Connections

Language Arts

Students may:

- Write stories about their pet and tell why the pet is important to them. Share their story with students in the lower grades.
- Write a poem about their favorite pet.

Science

Students may:

- Research how many unwanted animals can be produced by a pair of cats or dogs. Dog and cat overpopulation is a serious problem in the United States; the numbers are startling.
- Research what steps are being taken to control dog and cat overpopulation. Write to the American Society for the Prevention of Cruelty to Animals (ASPCA) and ask for free literature on spay and neuter programs.

Social Studies

Students may:

- Find out all they can about the stamp that draws attention to the problem of overpopulation of cats and dogs.

- Research all the major organizations that try to educate people about taking care of their pets.

Technology

Students may:

- Ask for free copies of the ASPCA's Animaland Pages, The Cat's Meow and Hot Diggity Dog, and then create their own newspaper or brochure with information about cats or dogs.

  Snack: Lozenges, egg-salad sandwiches, and punch

Annotated Titles About Dogs and Pets

Avi. *The Good Dog.* Atheneum Books for Young Readers, 2001.

McKinley is a Malamute, protector of his human pup, Jack, and head dog of Steamboat Springs. This story is told from McKinley's point of view. When the greyhound Duchess runs away from her owner who mistreats her, it is McKinley who must protect her in hiding. But what is he going to do about Lupin, a wolf, who has come to meet his pack and try to get the dogs to join up with him because his pack has become so small? "You could become a great dog. You could lead your whole pack to their liberation."

Branford, Henrietta. *Fire, Bed, and Bone.* Candlewick Press, 1998.

The setting of this historical fiction book is Medieval England, and it's told from the point of view of a loyal old hunting hound dog. He lives with his kind serf master, Rufus, and Rufus's wife, Comfort, who are taken prisoner for attending revolutionary meetings during the Peasant Revolt in 1381. The old dog rescues the children and sees to it that they are safe. When his master is taken prisoner, the cruelty of the times is demonstrated by how the dog and Rufus are both treated.

Bunting, Eve. *The Summer of Riley.* Scholastic Incorporated, 2001.

William's parents are divorced, his dad has a girlfriend, and his grandfather recently died. His mom takes him to the animal shelter to get a dog, and he selects a beautiful yellow lab named Riley. He brings Riley home and finds that he is well trained and loving. When William takes Riley to meet his neighbor and her old horse, Riley goes crazy, jumping fences to get at the horse. Then he barks and chases the horse until it collapses. In Oregon, it is a serious crime for dogs to chase and terrorize livestock and the Animal Control comes to take Riley. William is devastated and mounts a campaign to save Riley from being euthanized.

Byars, Betsy, Betsy Duffey, and Laurie Myers. *My Dog, My Hero.* Henry Holt and Company, 2000.

Betsy Byars and her daughters are dog lovers, and they collaborate for the first time to write this book. Eight dogs and their nominators are chosen to tell their stories to see who will win the My Hero title.

Choldenko, Gennifer. *Notes from a Liar and Her Dog.* Penguin Putnam Books for Young Readers, 2001.

Antonia McPherson is an experienced liar. Her mother always thinks she is wrong, her older sister makes fun of her best friend, and her younger sister is always tattling on her. Ant is devoted to her Chihuahua, Pistachio, and to her best friend, Harrison. A teacher finally sees the reason for Ant's lies, and her involvement precipitates a showdown between Ant and her mother.

Creech, Sharon. *Love That Dog: A Novel.* Joanna Cotler Books, 2001.

Gradually the story unfolds through poetry of a young boy and his yellow dog, Sky, who chases a ball into the street and is hit by a car and dies. Initially the boy resists poetry but eventually uses many famous poems and the inspiration of the poet Walter Dean Myers to help him write his own poem about Sky.

Gardiner, John R. *Stone Fox.* HarperCollins Children's Book Group, 1996.

Ten-year-old Willy must win the dogsled race to help save his grandfather's farm. The competition is stiff—Stone Fox is a huge Indian mountain man who is an experienced dogsled racer. But Willy's dog makes the ultimate sacrifice to help Willy win the race and save the farm.

Hausman, Gerald and Loretta. *Dogs of Myth: Tales from Around the World.* Simon & Schuster Books for Young Readers, 1999.

Here are thirteen myths about dogs from different cultures and divided into six chapters: The Creation Dog, Trickster Dog, Enchanted Dog, Guardian Dog, Super Dog, and The Treasure Dog

Henkes, Kevin. *Protecting Marie.* Greenwillow Books, 1995.

This is the story of a girl who always wanted a dog. Her father gives her a puppy but then takes it away after it ruins the house. Fanny is devastated by this and never trusts her father again. He is an older man and is going through some problems with his career as an artist. Eventually he gets Fanny another dog, and she lives in fear that he will take the dog away again. It turns out that the dog, Dinner, is helpful to her father's career.

Jacques, Brian. *Castaways of the Flying Dutchman.* Philomel Books, 2001.

The Flying Dutchman is a phantom ship condemned to sail the seas forever with its cruel Captain Vanderdecken and crew. In this story, there are two survivors of the curse, Ben and his dog Ned. An avenging angel spares them and thereafter they will be forever young and a force for good. In 1896 they find themselves in a small town in England, and it is up to them to save it from disaster.

Kehret, Peg. *Don't Tell Anyone.* Dutton Children's Books, 2000.

Megan discovers a group of feral cats living in a vacant lot. She brings them water and food every day and one day sees a sign that says the lot will soon be cleared for a new apartment building. Megan attempts to save the cats and in the process gets involved with a desperate criminal, is kidnapped, and must find her way back to safety.

Naylor, Phyllis Reynolds. *Saving Shiloh.* Econo-Clad, 1999.
This is the final story in the *Shiloh* trilogy and readers will see a change in Judd, whose past problems connect him to current robberies and even a murder. Marty defends Judd, seeing the change in him over time. In the end, Judd actually saves Shiloh from drowning and earns a hug from Marty.

——. *Shiloh Season.* Atheneum Books for Young Readers, 1996.
This is the second story in the *Shiloh* trilogy. Marty becomes increasingly concerned for Shiloh when Judd takes up drinking again and becomes reckless with his rifle.

——. *Shiloh.* Scott Foresman, 1991.
Eleven-year-old Marty lives with his poor family in the mountains of West Virginia. His neighbor, Judd, mistreats his dog, and Marty hides the dog to keep it safe. Marty's lies, omissions, and blackmail force a deal with Judd. Marty works for Judd to pay him for the dog, which Judd says he can keep. Marty's parents hear a different story from Marty.

Newkirk, Ingrid. *Kids Can Save the Animals: 101 Easy Things to Do.* Warner Books, 1991.
This book contains fascinating facts about animals and shares over 100 projects and ideas kids can do to help animals.

Newkirk, Ingrid, Linda McCartney & Cleveland Amory. *Save the Animals: 101 Easy Things You Can Do.* Warner Books, 1990.
This book tells many ways people can help prevent cruelty to animals. There are lots of simple and easy things for everyone to do.

Paulsen, Gary. *Puppies, Dogs, and Blue Northers: Reflections on Being Raised By a Pack of Sled Dogs.* Harcourt Brace and Company, 1996.
Gary Paulsen has a special relationship with his lead dog, Cookie. He is there when Cookie has her last litter and watches them grow from puppies to dogs, two of which would be leaders. One night, twenty-five miles into a run, with six of the young dogs in harness, they come to a train trestle. Someone has stolen the plywood from atop the trestle and the dogs suddenly stop. He can't turn them around. What will happen?

Rawls, Wilson. *Where the Red Fern Grows.* Bantam Books, 1997.
This is the story of Bill and his coonhound dogs and their adventures in the Ozarks. The threesome hunt raccoons and become quite successful. A confrontation with a mountain lion turns deadly and Billy learns about the old Native American legend of the sacred red ferns that grow over the graves of beloved dogs.

Taylor, Theodore. *The Trouble with Tuck.* Dell Yearling, 2000.
Helen's best friend, a beautiful golden Labrador named Friar Tuck, faces a great challenge. Helen discovers that Tuck is blind and focuses all her attention on helping Tuck overcome this devastating problem. Her solution for Tuck is unique and surprising.

——. *Tuck Triumphant.* Camelot, 1996.

In this sequel to *The Trouble with Tuck,* Helen's blind golden Labrador faces a new challenge when his Seeing Eye dog is tragically killed. Tuck uses all his senses to assist a terrified deaf orphan from Korea.

Additional Titles About Dogs and Pets

Alderton, David. *Dogs.* Dorling Kindersley, 1993.

American Kennel Club. *The Complete Dog Book.* Howell Book House, 1997.

Anderson, Laurie Halse. *Say Good-Bye.* Pleasant Company Publications, 2001.

——. *Fight for Life.* Pleasant Company Publications, 2000.

Armstrong, William Howard. *Sounder.* Harper & Row, 1969.

Avi. *The Good Dog.* Atheneum Books for Young Readers, 2001.

Booth, Martin. *War Dog: A Novel.* Aladdin Paperbacks, 1997.

Burnford, Sheila. *The Incredible Journey.* Little, Brown, 1961.

Calvert, Patricia. *Bigger.* Scribner, 1994.

——. *Sooner.* Atheneum Books for Young Readers, 1998.

Chan, Gillian. *The Carved Box.* Kids Can Press Ltd., 2001.

Cleary, Beverly. *Strider.* Morrow Junior Books, 1991.

Clutton-Brock, Juliet. *The Dog.* Dorling Kindersley, 2000.

Crisp, Marty. *Ratzo.* Northland Publishing, 1998.

——. *Private Captain: A Story of Gettysburg.* Penguin Putnam Books for Young Readers, 2001.

Dickinson, Peter. *Chuck and Danielle.* Bantam Doubleday Dell Books for Young Readers, 1996.

Fleischman, Sid. *Jim Ugly.* Greenwillow Books, 1992.

Gipson, Frederick Benjamin. *Old Yeller.* Harper & Row, 1956.

Gutman, Bill. *Adopting Pets: How to Choose Your New Best Friend.* Millbrook Press Inc., 2001.

Harlow, Joan H. *Star in the Storm.* Aladdin Paperbacks, 2001.

Hobbs, Will. *Wild Man Island.* HarperCollins Children's Book Group, 2002.

Jones, Diana Wynne. *Dogsbody.* HarperCollins Children's Book Group, 2001.

Kehret, Peg. *Shelter Dogs: Amazing Stories of Adopted Dogs.* Albert Whitman & Company, 1999.

Koller, Jackie French. *The Promise.* Bantam Doubleday Dell Books for Young Readers, 2001.

Levin, Betty. *Look Back, Moss.* HarperCollins Children's Book Group, 1999.

Lowry, Lois. *Stay!: Keeper's Story.* Houghton Mifflin Company, 1997.

———. *Anastasia, Absolutely.* Houghton Mifflin Company, 1995.

Marsden, John. *Checkers.* Bantam Doubleday Dell Books for Young Readers, 2000.

Mazer, Harry. *The Dog in the Freezer.* Simon & Schuster Children's Publishing, 1996.

McKay, Hillary. *Dog Friday.* Margaret K. McElderry, 1995.

Morey, Walt. *Kavik, the Wolf Dog.* Penguin Putnam Books for Young Readers, 1997.

O'Neill, Amanda. *Dogs.* Kingfisher, 2001.

Paterson, Katherine. *The Field of the Dogs.* HarperCollins Children's Book Group, 2001.

Paulsen, Gary. *My Life in Dog Years.* Delacorte Press, 1998.

Rosen, Michael J. *The Blessings of the Animals.* Farrar Straus Giroux, 2000.

Salisbury, Graham. *Jungle Dogs.* Delacorte Press, 1998.

Shalant, Phyllis. *The Great Eye.* Penguin Putnam Books for Young Readers, 1996.

Silverstein, Alvin. *Different Dogs.* Twenty-First Century Books, 2000.

Smith, Roland. *The Captain's Dog: My Journey with the Lewis and Clark Tribe.* Harcourt Brace and Company, 1999.

Strickland, Brad. *When Mack Came Back.* Penguin Putnam Books for Young Readers, 2000.

Talbert, Marc. *The Trap.* DK Publishing, Inc., 1999.

Tamar, Erika. *The Junkyard Dog.* Alfred A. Knopf, 1995.

Van de Velde, Vivian. *Smart Dog.* Bantam Doubleday Dell Books for Young Readers, 2000.

Van Draanen, Wendelin. *Sammy Keyes and the Runaway Elf.* Alfred A. Knopf, 1998.

Van Steenwyk, Elizabeth. *Three Dog Winter.* Bantam Doubleday Dell Books for Young Readers, 1999.

Wallace, Bill. *Running Wild.* Simon & Schuster Children's Publishing, 2000.

———. *Upchuck and the Rotten Willy.* Simon & Schuster Children's Publishing, 2000.

Weaver, Chap. *Bill.* Delacorte Press, 1994.

Westall, Robert. *The Kingdom by the Sea.* Farrar Straus Giroux, 1991.

Zinnen, Linda. *The Truth About Rats, Rules, and Seventh Grade.* HarperCollins Publishers, 2001.

Annotated Title by Kate DiCamillo

DiCamillo, Kate. *The Tiger Rising.* Candlewick Press, 2001.

Rob discovers a tiger in the woods behind the hotel where he moved just three months after his mother died. On the same day, he meets Sistine Bailey. They become friends and learn to trust and stand up for each other. What matters the most to them is the tiger and how they will set it free. The tiger is symbolic of the emotions Rob keeps hidden.

Teacher Resources About Dogs and Pets

Educators for Animal Rights and Humane Education (inactive, but provides an extensive List of Links for Educators)
http://www.e4ars.org
ASPCA Animal Lessons: Pet Population—Behind the Numbers, ASPCA, 2001.
ASPCA Humane Education Resource Guide for Teachers (order online)
http://www.aspca.org

Web Sites About Dogs and Pets

Pet Name Finder
http://ivillage.com/pets/petnames
The American Society for the Prevention of Cruelty to Animals
http://www.aspca.org
The Humane Society of the United States
http://www.hsus.org
Pet Adoption—Animal Shelters—Lost & Found
http://www.pets911.com
Alley Cat Allies: The National Feral Cat Resource
http://www.alleycat.org
Animal Planet
http://animal.discovery.com
PETA Kids
http://www.peta.org/kids/index.html
ASPCA's Animaland
http://www.animaland.org/

Web Sites About Kate DiCamillo

A Talk with Kate DiCamillo
http://www.kidsreads.com/authors/au-dicamillo-kate.asp
Kate DiCamillo
http://www.bookjackets.com/dicamillo/DiCamillo.html
2001 Newbery Honor Book Author Kate DiCamillo
http://f.about.com/z/js/spr03.htm
Author Profile: Kate DiCamillo
http://www.teenreads.com/authors/au-dicamillo-kate.asp

Prize-Winning Novelist Kate DiCamillo Depicts Joys, Pains of Kids' Lives
http://www.startribune.com/stories/1437/1638159.html

Contact Publisher:

Candlewick Press
2067 Massachusetts Avenue
Cambridge, MA 02140
http://www.candlewickpress.com

14

Lord of the Deep by Graham Salisbury
(Delacorte Press, 2001)

Genre: Values
Theme: Honesty and Values

Introduction

Character education is a necessary component of a student's education. In his own words, Graham Salisbury explores the decision-making process of his characters. Everyone faces difficult decisions, and reading about the potential and real consequences of such decisions might help in the future. Other interesting topics to explore include the Hawaiian Islands, deep-sea sport fishing, fishing lures, catch-and-release programs, and local fishing in your area. Play Hawaiian music or sea chanteys as background music. Decorate the room with a nautical or Hawaiian theme. Invite a local boat captain or fishing guide to discuss deep-sea fishing.

Summary of *Lord of the Deep*

Thirteen-year-old Mikey Donovan is delighted when his stepfather, Bill, asks him to help out with his boat, the Crystal-C, and his charter fishing business in the Hawaiian Islands. Mikey calls Bill the Lord of the Deep because he is an excellent deep-sea fisherman, strong, patient, kind, and loving to Mikey, his mom, and Mikey's blind little brother. Two tourists hire the boat and Mikey helps one of them capture a record-breaking mahi-mahi. Mikey's faith in Bill is shaken when the tourist makes a dishonest offer and Bill accepts.

Information About Graham Salisbury

Graham Salisbury comes from a 100-year line of newspapermen, all associated with Hawaii's morning paper, the *Honolulu Advertiser*. Although a career as a newsman could have been possible, Salisbury chose to imagine rather than report. "I enjoy writing about characters who might have been. To me, exploring fictional themes, situations, and lives is a quietly exhilarating experience. There are times when completely unexpected happenings take place as my fingertips walk the keyboard, things that make me laugh or get all choked up or even amaze me."

Salisbury's drive to write about the emotional journey kids must take to become adults in a challenging and complicated world is evident throughout his work. Says the author: "I've thought a lot about what my job is, or should be as an author of books for young readers. I don't write to teach, preach, lecture, or criticize, but to explore. And if my stories show characters choosing certain life options, and the possible consequences of having chosen those options, then I will have done something worthwhile."

His books—*Blue Skin of the Sea, Under the Blood-Red Sun, Shark Bait, Jungle Dogs, Lord of the Deep, Island Boyz*—and his short stories, too, have been celebrated widely with praise and distinguished awards. Graham Salisbury, winner of the PEN/Norma Klein Award, grew up on the islands of Oahu and Hawaii. Later he graduated from California State University, Northridge, and received an M.F.A. degree from Vermont College of Norwich University. He now is a faculty member of Vermont College's new M.F.A. program in Writing for Children.

Other important things to know about this author: He has worked as the skipper of a glass-bottom boat, as a deckhand on a deep-sea fishing boat, and as an elementary school teacher. His rock-and-roll band, The Millennium, had a number-one hit in the Philippines. He once surfed with a shark, got stung by a Portuguese man-of-war, and swam for his life from a moray eel. Believe it or not, he didn't wear shoes until the sixth grade, and he never saw snow until he was nineteen. Graham Salisbury now lives with his family in Portland, Oregon.

Discussion Questions

- Describe Mikey's family.
- What are the characteristics of a good father?
- How does Mikey's mother encourage the relationship between Mikey and Bill?
- What does Mikey learn about honesty?
- What does Bill have to say about honesty?
- Why does Bill want Mikey to forgive his dad?
- Why is it so difficult to forgive? Is it important to forgive?
- Does communication have anything to do with forgiveness?
- How does Mikey deal with fear? How do you deal with fear?
- How does Mikey come of age in this novel? What does coming of age mean to you?

Content Area Connections

Language Arts

Students may:

- Write a letter to Mikey's father.
- Create a ship's log of the things that happened each day on an imaginary deep-sea fishing trip.

Social Studies

Students may:
- Work in seven groups and research and report on one of the Hawaiian Islands.

Science

Students may:

- Study the weather conditions around the Hawaiian Islands. How do these conditions affect deep sea fishing?
- Study Hawaiian fishing lures: http://www.hawaiianfishinglures.com. Create a poster matching the lures to the fish. What are the differences between hand-tied and machine-made lures?

Art

Students may:

- Create a travel brochure/advertisement for their deep-sea fishing boat trips.
- Create a collage of all the different types of fish that live in the Pacific Ocean around the Hawaiian Islands.

Technology

Students may:

- Research Hawaii and deep-sea fishing on the Internet. Create a presentation of what they find.
- Learn about Catch and Release Conservation Programs by searching the Internet.

Mapping

Students may:

- Map all the words they can think of that describe a father.
- Map all the words they can think of that have to do with fishing and boats.

Snack: Macadamia nuts, pineapple, papaya, goldfish crackers

Annotated Titles About Honesty and Values

Avi. *Nothing But the Truth.* Avon Books, 1991.

Phillip is looking for a way to get transferred out of Miss Narwin's homeroom and English class. Phillip did not fulfill the requirements of his English class, so he received a D, which meant he could not be on the track team. Phillip convinced himself that Miss Narwin did not like him. After the morning announcements, students are asked to rise and stand at respectful, silent attention during the playing of the national anthem. Phillip begins humming and continues in spite of Miss Narwin's request for silence. Phillip insists he is not disrespectful when he is "singing" the national anthem and he wants to be transferred out of her homeroom and English class. How far is Phillip willing to press this issue?

Cormier, Robert. *The Chocolate War.* Pantheon Books, 1974.

Jerry has a poster of a solitary man standing upright on the beach mounted inside his locker. Inscribed on the poster is the slogan: "Do I Dare Disturb the Universe." Jerry comes to understand the poster when he defies a teacher, the Vigils (an underground organization), and ultimately the entire school. He sadly learns that people only let you do your own thing when it happens to be their own thing.

DeClements, Barthe. *Liar, Liar.* Marshall Cavendish, 1998.

Gretchen Griswald lives with her dad, and her three brothers (one step-brother) live with her mom. She has a good friend named Susan November and gets along well at school until a new girl, Marybelle, moves into town. Marybelle starts telling tales about the teacher and classmates. Soon the girls she likes most are snubbing Gretchen. Her brother helps her get to the bottom of the problem.

Griffin, Adele. *Amandine.* Hyperion Books for Children, 2001.

Delia recently moved from New York mid-year and is in the ninth grade. Delia is overweight, shy, and feels that she never does anything right in her parents' eyes. Delia takes items from people she likes in hopes that a part of what they have will become a part of her. Delia meets Amandine the last day of her first week of school. Amandine is part artist, part ballet dancer, and part actress. Amandine plays dangerous games and senses Delia's loneliness and manipulates her. Delia tells Amandine lies that will come back to haunt her. Amandine also tell lies, and when Delia has enough courage to break Amandine's hold over her, Amandine seeks revenge by telling a lie about Delia's father.

Naidoo, Beverley. *The Other Side of Truth.* HarperCollins Publishers, 2000.

Sade and Femi witness their mother's death in Nigeria. Their father, a reporter, has been threatened because of his outspoken opinions. Sade and Femi are smuggled illegally to London and encounter many frightening experiences when the uncle they are supposed to stay with mysteriously disappears.

Nolan, Peggy. *The Spy Who Came in from the Sea.* Pineapple Press, 1999.

During World War II, Francis moves to Jacksonville, Florida, to be near his dad, but unbeknownst to Frank and his mother, Pops was shipped out on an aircraft carrier. Frank's mom gets a job in the shipbuilding yard and they rent a "chicken coop" just off the beach. At his new school, Frank earns a reputation for exaggerating the truth. One evening Frank observes a submarine momentarily stuck on a sandbar and a raft with a man climbing out of it into the surf. The man staggers up the beach and buries a chest in the sand before he makes his way to the main road. Frank is sure he just witnessed a spy being dropped off on the beach, but how will he convince others that this time he is not "crying wolf?" Sunshine State Young Reader Award Nominee 2001–02.

Oates, Joyce Carol. *Big Mouth & Ugly Girl.* HarperCollins Children's Books, 2002.

"Big Mouth" Matt Donaghy gets a three-day suspension when someone reports that he threatened to blow up the school if his play wasn't accepted for the arts festival. Ursula Riggs, who calls herself Ugly Girl, heard what Matt said and came to his defense despite warnings from her mother about getting involved. Matt is shut out by his former friends and begins an awkward friendship with Ugly Girl. When Matt's family decides to sue the school and his accusers, things almost get out of hand.

Truth & Lies: An Anthology of Poems. Edited by Patrice Vecchione. Henry Holt and Company, 2001.

"Lies can be used to hurt, manipulate, or to protect.... Poetry is a particular way of telling the truth." Read, feel, and absorb the poems about truth and lies from different time periods and cultures.

Additional Titles About Honesty and Values

Amos, Janine. *Admitting Mistakes.* Gareth Stevens, Inc., 2002.
Bawdin, Nina. *Humbug.* Clarion Books, 1992.
Bennett, William J. *The Book of Virtues: A Treasury of Great Moral Stories.* Simon & Schuster Trade, 1993.
Bowen, Fred. *Winners Take All.* Peachtree Publishers, Ltd., 2000.
Cadnum, Michael. *Rundown.* Penguin Putnam Books for Young Readers, 2001.
Coville, Bruce. *The Skull of Truth: A Magic Shop Book.* Harcourt Children's Books, 1997.
DeClements, Barthe. *Five Finger Discount.* Delacorte Press, 1989.
Hurwitz, Johanna. *The Cold & Hot Winter.* Morrow Junior Books, 1988.
Koss, Amy Goldman. *Smoke Screen.* Pleasant Company Publications, 2000.
Lowry, Lois. *Your Move, J.P.* Houghton Mifflin Company, 1990.
McDonald, Joy. *Shades of Gray.* Random House Children's Publishing, 2001.
Pearson, Mary E. *Scribbler of Dreams.* Harcourt Children's Books, 2001.
Seidler, Tor. *Terpin.* HarperCollins Children's Book Group, 2002.
Tomey, Ingrid. *Nobody Else Has to Know.* Random House, Inc., 1999.
Woods, Ron. *The Hero.* Alfred A. Knopf Books for Young Readers, 2001.

Annotated Titles by Graham Salisbury

Blue Skin of the Sea: A Novel in Stories. Laurel-Leaf Books, 1994.
Eleven short stories follow the lives of Sonny Mendoza and his cousin Keo, young men who grow up in a Hawaiian fishing village between 1953 and 1966, and their families and friends.

Island Boyz. Delacorte Press, 2002.
This is a collection of short stories set in Hawaii. The book begins with a free-verse poem about the varied types of boys living on the islands and what it meant to be one of the boyz. The stories are written in the first person and deal with issues, feelings, and island life.

Jungle Dogs. Laurel-Leaf Books, 1999.
"Boy" Regis finds it difficult to take a stand for himself because his older brother always gets involved in his problems and teases him for being weak. Boy must find a way to prove his courage by facing the pack of wild dogs that threatens his paper route.

Shark Bait. Delacorte Press, 1997.

Mokes's dad is a policeman and he makes it clear to Mokes that he doesn't want him in town the night a ship is in port because there might be trouble when all the sailors come ashore. But this is the night when Booley is going to fight one of the sailors to settle a score, and Mokes and his buddies do not want to miss the action. Mokes disobeys and inadvertently provides one of Booley's friends with a gun, and the situation almost turns deadly.

Under the Blood-Red Sun. Delacorte Press, 1994.

This book was the winner of the Scott O'Dell Award for Historical Fiction. Set in Hawaii, it tells the story of Tomi and his Japanese American family just before the bombing of Pearl Harbor in 1941 and the racism, violence, and hardships they suffer as a result.

Teacher Resources About Honesty and Values

Borba, Michelle. *Building Moral Intelligence: The Seven Essential Virtues That Teach Kids to Do the Right Thing.* Jossey-Bass, 2001.

Findlay, Diane. *Characters with Character: Using Children's Literature in Character Education.* Alleyside Press, 2001.

Greer, Colin and Herbert Kohl. *A Call to Character: A Family Treasury of Stories, Poems, Plays, Proverbs, and Fables to Guide the Development of Values for You and Your Children.* HarperPerennial, 1995.

Kilpatrick, William, Gregory Wolfe, and Suzanne Wolfe. *Books That Build Character: A Guide to Teaching Your Child Moral Values Through Stories.* Touchtone Book, 1994.

Web Sites About Hawaiian Islands

Hawaiian Islands Recent Marine Data
http://www.ndbc.noaa.gov/Maps.Hawaii.shtml
Ocean Explorers—Northwestern Hawaiian Islands
http://oceanexplorer.noaa.gov/explorations/02hawaii/welcome.html
Big Game Fishing—Oahu, Hawaii Deep Sea Fishing Charters
http://www.kuuloakai.com/your_charter.asp
Hawaiian Fishing Lures
http://www.hawaiifishinglures.com

Web Sites About Graham Salisbury

Graham Salisbury's Place
http://www.grahamsalisbury.com
Authors and Illustrators: Graham Salisbury
http://www.randomhouse.com/teachers/authors/sals.html

"Writing My Way Home": An Interview with Graham Salisbury
http://scholar.lib.vt.edu/ejournals/ALAN/winter97/w97–03-Benton.html
Interview with Children's and Young Adult Book Author Graham Salisbury
http://www.cynthialeitichsmith.com/auth-illGrahamSalisbury.htm
Hang with the Authors—Graham Salisbury
http://www.randomhouse.com/teens/gsalisbury.html
An Interview with Graham Salisbury at Amazon.com
http://www.amazon.com/exec/obidos/show-interview/
s-g-alisburyraham/103–0985017–1568642

Contact Publisher:

Random House Children's Books
1540 Broadway
New York, NY 10036
http://www.randomhouse.com/teachers

Graham Salisbury
112 Third Street
Lake Oswego, OR 97034
graham@grahamsalisbury.com

15

Monster by Walter Dean Myers (HarperCollins Publishers, 1999)

Genre: Realistic Fiction
Theme: Crime and Moviemaking

Introduction

Walter Dean Myers was the first recipient of the Michael L. Printz Award for Young Adult Readers. This chapter could be used during January or February in conjunction with major book award announcements and Black History month. Walter Dean Myers has written numerous books, and students who like *Monster* might be led to read his autobiography, *Bad Boy,* or *Now Is Your Time: The African American Struggle for Freedom.* *Monster* is a thought-provoking quick read. The movie-script format of the book grabs readers' attention and should produce conversations as to its effectiveness. *Monster* will generate interest in such topics as moviemaking, movie scripting, profiling, prison life, crime, and Civil Rights.

Summary of *Monster*

Sixteen-year-old Steve Harmon is on trial for felony murder. The prosecutor calls him a monster because of his role in the murder of a convenience store owner. But was Steve really the lookout for those involved in a robbery, or was he simply in the wrong place at the wrong time? Steve is an aspiring film writer, so he records his impressions of the trial, the crime scene, and his jail time in movie-script format alternating with journal entries—presented in a "handwritten" font in the book.

Information About Walter Dean Myers

Walter Dean Myers was born in 1937 in West Virginia. He grew up in Harlem in the 1940s and 1950s, when writing was not a typical career

path for black children. Myers joined the army when he turned 17. He
had a variety of jobs over the years, but he always found time to write.
Myers is the author of many highly acclaimed books, including *Scorpions,*
a 1989 Newbery Honor Book; *Now Is Your Time: The African-American
Struggle for Freedom,* winner of the 1992 Coretta Scott King Author Award;
The Mouse Rap, an ALA Best Book for Young Adults; and *Brown Angels: An
Album of Pictures and Verse.* In 1994, he received the ALA's Margaret A. Edwards Award for lifetime achievement in writing for young adults. Myers
lives in New Jersey with his family.

Discussion Questions

- When does Steve lose control of his own fate?
- What could Steve have done differently to avoid the situation?
- Why does Steve begin to doubt himself?
- What usually happens with witnesses? Why can witnesses' stories sometime
  be so different?
- Is Steve innocent or guilty? Can there be varying degrees of guilt?
- How does the screenplay format enhance the story?
- The beginning credits are reminiscent of *Star Wars.* What does that tell you
  about Steve?
- What does this story tell readers about choices we make?
- Is there a lesson to be learned from this story?
- Would you recommend this book to a friend? Why or why not?

Content Area Connections

Language Arts

Students may:

- Write a screenplay. Select a favorite story, write out a list of characters, list the
  places the story takes place. Divide the action of the story into three or four acts
  based on natural transitions within the story. Describe in detail the scene
  where each act will take place. Convert the story action into dialogue form.
  Lastly, stage the play!

Social Studies

Students may:

- Use the Web site http://www.filmsite.org and research the history of movies.
  Look at all the "greatest" lists and write up the top ten from a category that interests them.

- Research African American illustrators. Prepare a report, poster, or display about some of them, their works, and their lives.

Science

Students may:

- Explore how forensic science is used in criminal investigations. Stage a classroom crime—complete with a footprint, a hand-written note, a hair sample, a fingerprint, a thread from clothing.
- Do some research on the history of forensic science in the United States. Share their findings with the class.

Technology

Students may:

- Use the Internet to explore current trends in moviemaking. Create a presentation about the film industry.

Art

Students may:

- Make a billboard to advertise the new play in town: *Monster.*

Snack: Popcorn, movie candy

Annotated Titles About Crime and Moviemaking

Allison, Anthony. *Hear These Voices: Youth at the Edge of the Millennium.* Dutton Children's Books, 1999.

These are fifteen at-risk young adults from around the world who have faced their responsibilities and share their stories of survival, health, safety, food, and shelter.

Atkin, S. Beth. *Voices from the Streets.* Little, Brown, 1996.

Why do kids join gangs? How can they get out of gangs? These are the topics discussed in interviews with former gang members from various areas of the United States. Striking photos, poems, information on how to help, a list of intervention programs, a glossary, and a list of recommended books are included.

Barr, Roger. *Juvenile Crime.* Lucent Books, 1998.

This book defines juvenile crime and current trends. It also reviews the juvenile justice system. The book discusses punishment and prevention. It includes a list of organizations to contact and suggestions for additional reading.

Cormier, Robert. *The Rag and Bone Shop.* Delacorte Press, 2001.

Twelve-year-old Jason was the last to see his seven-year-old neighbor alive. She was brutally murdered, her body found in the woods, covered with leaves. It is a high-profile case and there is no evidence, but the police call in a well-known interrogator named Trent who always gets a confession. When Jason meets Trent, he thinks he is helping. His father is away on a business trip, and his mother lets him go off with the police, assuring him he has a duty to assist. The end results are devastating for both Trent and Jason.

Gallo, Edward R., ed. *On the Fringe.* Dial Books, 2001.

"This book is dedicated to every kid who has ever been called a hurtful name. And to every kid who has tried to feel superior by putting down someone else." Eleven young adult authors were invited to write for this anthology about middle and high school students who do not fit into the norm. Includes authors such as Ron Koertge, Jack Gann, Graham Salisbury, Alden R. Carter, Joan Bauer, and Chris Crutcher.

Sachar, Louis. *Holes.* Farrar Straus Giroux, 1998.

Stanley Yelnats IV's great grandfather lost his entire fortune and a curse is placed on his descendants. Our Stanley continues to have bad luck. He is sent to Camp Green Lake for a crime he didn't commit. Camp Green Lake is not at all what its name suggests. It is desolate and barren with no water in sight, so fences and guards are unnecessary. His punishment is to dig a hole five feet by five feet in width and depth every day in the hot sun before he is allowed to do anything else. Everything changes when Stanley finds a small gold tube with the initials KB. *Holes* won the Newbery Award in 1999.

Strasser, Todd. *Give a Boy a Gun.* Simon Pulse, 1999.

This is the story of two boys, Gary Searle and Brendan Lawlor, who hold students hostage in a gym with automatic weapons and homemade bombs. Gary's stepsister, Denise Shipley, arrives home after the tragedy to interview friends, neighbors, teachers, and students to try to find out how and why this happened. Additional facts and statistics about guns and their use are found throughout, set apart by a dotted line and smaller type. The author states in the Author's Note, "The story you are about to read is a work of fiction. Nothing—and everything— about it is real."

Walter, Virginia. *Making Up Megaboy.* Bantam Books, 1999.

Robbie Jones took the gun from his father's sock drawer and killed Mr. Koh. Mr. Koh was the owner of the Main Street Liquor Store. Was this a random act of violence, or was Robbie assuming the role of Megaboy and defending Taragirl from danger? Many people who know Robbie offer their opinions as to why this happened when there was no apparent motive. The graphics are an integral part of this unusual book. It's a quick read that will foster discussion on a timely topic.

Additional Titles About Crime and Moviemaking

Aaseng, Nathan. *You Are the Juror.* Oliver Press, 1997.

Bode, Janet. *Hard Tim: A Real Life Look at Juvenile Crime and Violence.* Delacorte Press, 1996.

Brookis, Kevin. *Martyn Pig.* Scholastic Incorporated, 2002.

Cadnum, Michael. *Edge.* Viking Press, 1997.

Cozic, Charles P., ed. *America's Prisons: Opposing Viewpoints.* Greenhaven Press, 1997.

Cross, Robin. *Movie Magic: A Behind-the-Scenes Look at Filmmaking.* Sterling Publishing Company, 1996.

DeHahn, Tracee and Austin Sarat. *Crimes Against Children: Child Abuse and Neglect.* Chelsea House Publishers, 2000.

Frantz, John P. *Video Cinema: Techniques and Projects for Beginning Filmmakers.* Chicago Review Press, 1994.

Gardner, Robert. *Crime Lab 101: Experimenting with Crime Detection.* Walker, 1992.

Giberga, Jane Sughrue. *Friends to Die For.* Dial Books, 1997.

Goodwin, William. *Teen Violence.* Lucent Books, 1998.

Hamilton, Jake. *Special Effects in Film and Television.* DK Publishing, Inc., 1998.

History of Moviemaking: Animation and Live-Action, from Silent to Sound, Black and White to Color. Scholastic Incorporated, 1995.

Karson, Jill, ed. *Criminal Justice: Opposing Viewpoints.* Greenhaven Press, 1998.

Kaye, Marilyn. *Pursuing Amy.* Turtleback Books, 1999.

Kehret, Peg. *Don't Tell Anyone.* Dutton Children's Books, 2000.

Kim, Henny H., ed. *Youth Violence.* Greenhaven Press, 1998.

Kuklin, Susan. *Trial: The Inside Story.* Henry Holt and Company, 2001.

Lane, Brian. *Crime and Detection.* Alfred A. Knopf, 1998.

Levitin, Sonia. *Yesterday's Child.* Simon & Schuster Books for Young Readers, 1997.

O'Brien, Lisa. *Lights, Camera, Action! Making Movies and TV from the Inside Out.* Owl Books, 1998.

O'Neill, Terry. *Gun Control.* Greenhaven Press, 2000.

Parkinson, David. *The Young Oxford Book of the Movies.* Oxford University Press, 1996.

Philbrick, Rodman. *The Last Book in the Universe.* Scholastic Incorporated, 2000.

Pierce, Tamora. *Tandry's Book.* Scholastic Incorporated, 1999.

Powell, Phelan. *Major Unsolved Crimes.* Chelsea House Publishers, 2000.

Rodowsky, Colby. *Remembering Mog.* Farrar Straus Giroux, 1996.

Roleff, Tamara L. *Crime and Criminals.* Gale Group, 2001.

Silverstein, Herma. *Kids Who Kill.* Twenty-First Century Books, 1997.

Skinner, David. *Thundershine: Tales of Metakids.* Simon & Schuster Children's Publishing, 1999.

Smith, Roland. *Zack's Lie.* Hyperion Books for Children, 2001.

Stevenson, James. *The Unprotected Witness.* Greenwillow Books, 1997.

Williams, Stanley T. *Live in Prison.* SeaStar Books, 2001.

Woodson, Jacqueline. *Hush.* Penguin Putnam, Incorporated, 2002.

Annotated Titles by Walter Dean Myers

145th Street Short Stories. Delacorte Press, 2000.
Ten stories about young people and adults who live on one block in Harlem. Some of the stories are happy and some are sad, but violence and love are a constant.

Amistad. Penguin Putnam Books for Young Readers, 1998.
In 1839 there was a rebellion on the slave ship Amistad. In a bloody struggle, the African captives aboard rebelled against their kidnappers and declared mutiny. While trying to sail the ship home, the Africans accidentally ended up in New York. They were later imprisoned and put on trial for murder.

Bad Boy: A Memoir. HarperCollins Juvenile Books, 2001.
Walter Dean Myers grew up in the 1940s in Harlem, always wanting to be a writer and discovering it was difficult to be Black, poor, and a reader. He was physically big, aggressive, hot-tempered, and had a speech defect and thus was always in trouble and truant. He did have some teachers along the way who realized his writing ability and encouraged him, but he eventually dropped out of high school, joined the army, and then had a series of menial jobs before he became serious about writing.

Darnell Rock Reporting. Delacorte Press, 1994.
Darnell Rock is not doing well at school. He is given one last opportunity to get his act together and becomes a reporter for the school newspaper. He is amazed to discover that he can make a difference in the school community.

The Glory Field. Scholastic Incorporated, 1995.
This is the story of five generations in an African American family. It begins with the first one, who was captured and became a slave, through the Civil War and the end of segregation, to problems at a family reunion.

The Greatest: Muhammad Ali. Scholastic Press, 2001.
When Cassius Clay was twelve years old, his Schwinn bicycle was stolen. He reported it to a policeman, Joe Martin, saying that when he found the person who stole it, he would beat him up. Joe Martin, the policeman, also taught boxing. Cassius started boxing lessons and soon was training six days a week. When he was eighteen, he went to Rome and participated in and won the lightweight division in the Olympics. Who was this brash, good-looking young Black man? Cassius Clay had lightning hand and foot speed. His technique was "float like a butterfly, sting like a bee!" Cassius Clay would prove to be the Greatest Athlete of the Twentieth Century, as stated by *Sports Illustrated.* He would test his strength of conviction and influence the political, racial, and religious atmosphere of the 1960s and 1970s.

Handbook for Boys. HarperCollins Children's Book Group, 2002.
The book begins with a judge giving 16-year-old Jimmy the option of being assigned to a juvenile facility for six months for assaulting a classmate or to a com-

munity-mentoring program. Of course he chooses the latter and begins his relationship with Duke Wilson, the owner of a neighborhood barbershop where he will work every day after school. Duke is an older man who, with several of his cronies, tries to give Jimmy and Kevin (another troubled youth) advice about the decisions and paths they will choose as they travel through life.

Harlem. Scholastic Press, 1997.
Many interesting facts about art, music, people, and everyday life in Harlem are expressed in this poem. It is a Caldecott Honor Book and winner of the Coretta Scott King Award. Bright, bold pictures contribute to the reader's understanding of life in Harlem.

The Journal of Joshua Loper: A Black Cowboy. Scholastic Incorporated, 1999.
An African American boy goes on his first cattle drive and grapples with racial prejudices.

Malcolm X: By Any Means Necessary. Scholastic Incorporated, 1993.
The story of Malcolm X and his civil rights struggles from his childhood through his time in prison to his position as leader of the Nation of Islam.

One More River to Cross: An African American Photo Album. Harcourt Children's Books, 1995.
A collection of photographs that show the history of Black Americans.

Patrol: An American Soldier in Vietnam. HarperCollins Publishers, 2002.
This story-poem tells about a frightened American soldier in the Vietnam jungles. He is ready to shoot but has no idea where his enemy is. He asks when it will all be over and is very glad to be alive at the end of the day. Ann Grifalconi's brilliant collages add to the haunting story. Walter Dean Myers's brother was killed in the Vietnam War in 1968.

Scorpions. HarperTrophy, 1988.
Jamal's brother Randy is in prison and he wants Jamal, who is twelve, to take control of the Scorpions. Mack, who was Randy's ace, gives Jamal a gun so Jamal will gain a new level of respect from his enemies. Jamal is caught up in gangs and violence.

Smiffy Blue: Ace Crime Detective: The Case of the Missing Ruby and Other Stories. Scholastic Incorporated, 1996.
Smiffy Blue, an African American detective with a slapstick style, has a new approach to solving crimes. Readers find clues hidden in the humorous two-color illustrations.

The Story of Three Kingdoms. HarperCollins Publishers, 1995.
A fable about the People and how they used storytellers and the influence of the spoken word to control the three kingdoms: earth, sea, and sky.

Young Martin's Promise. Raintree Steck-Vaughn Publishers, 1993.
The story of the life of Martin Luther King, Jr., the changes he initiated, and why we celebrate his birthday.

Teacher Resources About Crime and Moviemaking

Kyker, Keith and Christopher Curchy. *Television Production: A Classroom Approach.* Libraries Unlimited, 1993.

——. *Television Production for Elementary and Middle Schools.* Libraries Unlimited, 1994.

Lipschultz, Andy. *How the Grinch Stole Hollywood: The Making of the Movie.* Random House, 2000.

O'Neill, Rory and Eden Muir. *Start Here: Movie Making with iMovie.* OnWord Press, 2001.

An excellent introduction to filmmaking. Provides opportunities to gain first-hand experience in every aspect of the moviemaking process, from purchasing equipment and gaining a working knowledge of photography and film basics through sketching a storyboard and developing an original movie idea.

Shaw, James E. *Jack & Jill: Why They Kill: Saving Our Children, Saving Ourselves.* Onjinjinkta Publishing, 2000.

This is a guide for parents and teachers about adolescents and violence. It addresses bullies, depression, loneliness, and alienation in adolescents. It provides suggestions for making changes, for raising a well-balanced child, and parenting help in general.

Web Sites About Crime and Moviemaking

How Are Hollywood Films Made?
http://www.learner.org/exhibits/cinema/
Attack of the 50-foot Chicken
http://www.pbs.org/wgbh/nova/specialfx2/green.html
Wordplayer for Screenwriters
http://www.wordplayer.com/welcome.html
Ojai, CA Film Festival
http://www.filmfestival.ojai.net/youth.htm
Film 101 from HBO's 30 by 30
http://www.hbomagnet.com/cree8/30x30/cmp/navindex.html
Admit One's Filmmaking Tips from the Pros
http://familyscreenscene.allinfoabout.com/features/admitone.html
FX: The Art of Movie Magic
http://familyscreenscene.allinfoabout.com/features/fx.html
Nick Corirossi: Teen Film Maker
http://familyscreenscene.allinfoabout.com/features/cori.html
Script Writing
http://www.storiestogrowby.com/newscripts_body.html

Web Sites About Walter Dean Myers

Learning About Walter Dean Myers
http://scils.rutgers.edu/ ~kvander/myers.html
Walter Dean Myers
http://www.edupaperback.org/authorbios/Myers_WalterDean.html
Walter Dean Myers—Biography and Interview
http://www.teenreads.com/authors/au-myers-walterdean.asp
Authors and Illustrators—Walter Dean Myers
http://www.randomhouse.com/teachers/authors/myer.html
Margaret A. Edwards Award Winner—Walter Dean Myers
http://www.carr.lib.md.us/mae/myer/myers.htm
Meet the Author—Walter Dean Myers
http://www.eduplace.com/kids/hmr/mtai/wdmyers.html
Walter Dean Myers
http://aalbc.com/authors/walter1.htm

Contact Publisher:

HarperCollins Children's Books
1350 Avenue of the Americas
New York, NY 10019
http://www.harperchildrens.com/schoolhouse

Annotated Professional Resources

Allen, Janet and Kyle Gonzalez. *There's Room for Me Here: Literacy Workshop in the Middle School.* Stenhouse, 1998.

This book is about the literacy classroom of a middle school teacher who helps struggling readers. The book provides information on establishing a literacy workshop; selecting and using effective resources; implementing appropriate record-keeping; helping students establish goals; using read-alouds and shared, guided, and independent reading; and helping students become effective content-area readers. The book includes useful forms and extensive bibliographies.

Ammon, Bette D. and Gale W. Sherman. *Worth a Thousand Words: An Annotated Guide to Picture Books for Older Readers.* Libraries Unlimited, 1996.

The authors include annotated picture books with universal themes to be used with older students. Each picture-book description has in the margins the subject, themes, and genre. The book also includes suggestions on how you might use it with your curriculum. Only includes books published prior to 1995.

Atwell, Nancie. *In the Middle: New Understandings About Writing, Reading, and Learning.* Heinemann, 1998.

Certainly the most important book for any middle level teacher to have. The chapters include how to teach reading and writing, making the best of adolescence, mini-lessons, responses, and evaluating. The book is filled with samples of student work and appendixes rich with charts, surveys, checklists, records, and other useful reproducibles.

Billmeyer, Rachel and Mary Lee Barton. *Teaching Reading in the Content Areas: If Not Me, Then Who?* McREL (Mid-Continent Research for Education and Learning), 1998.

A graphic organizer showing the three interactive elements of reading and the six assumptions about learning introduces this book. It goes on to discuss each element and assumption. The book ends with a complete and useful bibliography. This is an excellent resource filled with strategies for all content-area teachers who know the importance of reading and want to help their students read more effectively.

Bullock, Richard, ed. *Why Workshop? Changing Course in 7–12 English.* Stenhouse, 1998.

This book has nine essays written by experienced teachers. There is information on using writing and reading workshops as the primary organization method for language arts classrooms. One essay deals with responses to literature and offers useful suggestions. The book includes a very complete workshop course plan.

Calkins, Lucy. *The Art of Teaching Reading.* Addison-Wesley Longman, 2000.
This book encompasses all phases of the teaching of reading, including independent reading, guided reading, reading aloud, word study, booktalks, mini-lessons, writing about reading, and much more.

Chatton, Barbara and Lynn Decker Collins. *Blurring the Edges: Integrated Curriculum through Writing and Children's Literature.* Heinemann, 1999.
The authors provide possibilities for combining subjects, themes, and genres. The index at the back of the book is divided by authors, titles, and subjects. The chapters deal with the writing process and reading and writing across the curriculum. There are thematic units on mystery, magic and history, letters and diaries, math, science, and textures. Each section has annotated lists of children's books that inform and support children's studies.

Daniels, Harvey. *Literature Circles: Voice and Choice in the Student-Centered Classroom.* Stenhouse, 1994.
Everything you need to know about literature circles—getting started, managing groups, finding materials, record-keeping, evaluating and grading, problems, questions, and variations—for all levels from primary grades through college.

Herz, Sarah K. with Donald R. Gallo. *From Hinton to Hamlet: Building Bridges Between Young Adult Literature and the Classics.* Greenwood Press, 1996.
The value of young-adult literature lies in its ability to draw students' attention into the story immediately because it deals with problems in their own lives. Young-adult literature gives students the right to experience reading as a pleasurable activity and helps them become competent readers. The following are unique characteristics of young-adult literature: main character is a teenager; events, problems, plots are related to teens; dialogue reflects teenage speech; point of view is from an adolescent's perspective; the novel is short; and the actions and decisions of the main characters are major factors in the outcome of the conflict. It is suggested that young-adult literature should be an important part of literature classes because it can be used as a bridge to the classics.

Hill, Bonnie Campbell, Katherine L. Schlick Noe, and Nancy Johnson. *Literature Circles Resource Guide: Teaching Suggestions, Forms, Sample Book Lists, and Database.* Christopher-Gordon Publishers, Inc., 2001.
This book comes with a CD of titles and forms and is a great resource for organizing literature circles in all grade levels.

Jackson, Norma with Paula Pillow. *The Reading-Writing Workshop: Getting Started.* Scholastic Professional Books, 1992.
All the necessary details for setting up a reading/writing workshop are covered in this book. It includes information on what the workshop is, how it works, and how students and teachers keep track of work. Reproducible forms are provided for making management easier. There is a chapter on organizing the classroom and suggestions for literature focus and skill lessons, projects, and themes. There is also an extensive bibliography of professional and children's books.

Knowles, Elizabeth and Martha Smith. *The Reading Connection: Bringing Parents, Teachers and Librarians Together.* Libraries Unlimited, 1997.

Establishing a book club is a great way to involve parents in promoting literacy to young readers. This book shows you how to start a book club in your school or community, and it provides bibliographies of literature resources for children in grades K–8. Suggested topics and sample book club sessions help you get started, and the extensive bibliography, arranged by genre, can guide parents and students in selecting reading material. Chapters cover read-alouds, picture books, horror stories, multicultural literature, poetry, science fiction, nonfiction and reference, bibliotherapy and problem novels, award-winning books, biographies, and books in a series. For each genre, the authors offer a general overview, suggest discussion questions, provide a bibliography, and list resources for further reading. Helpful Internet addresses and additional topics are in the concluding chapter.

———. *More Reading Connections: Bringing Parents, Teachers, and Librarians Together.* Libraries Unlimited, 1999.

Great topics and sample book club sessions help you start a book club and keep it going. Chapters cover humor, families, social issues, folklore and mythology, sports, magazines, picture books as art, censorship, the Internet, middle school readers, gender bias, booktalks, and the arts. For each genre, the authors offer a general overview, discussion questions, a bibliography, resources for further reading, and appropriate Web sites. If you want to promote literacy and involve parents in the reading program, you'll love this book and its companion, *The Reading Connection.*

———. *Reading Rules! Motivating Teens to Read.* Libraries Unlimited, 2001.

This is a guide for encouraging teenagers to read more and read more enthusiastically. Supported by fascinating background statistics and data, this book addresses the challenges of motivating teens to read through a framework by which educators can create a reading plan for their school. Each individual chapter can be used as a discussion generator or a workshop as needed to improve the overall reading program for young adults. There are chapters on reading workshops, book clubs, booktalks, literature circles, thematic units, and information literacy. These chapters suggest ways to incorporate these activities into the classroom or media center and provide extensive lists of sample materials, including annotations on appropriate resources for student reading and professional development.

Langer, Judith. *Envisioning Literature: Literary Understanding and Literature Instruction.* Teachers College Press, 1995.

Interacting with texts, literary discussions, strategies for teaching, literature for students the system has failed, literary concepts and vocabulary, and literature across the curriculum are some of the topics discussed in this book about literature for middle and high school students.

Means, Beth and Lindy Lindner. *Teaching Writing in Middle School: Tips, Tricks, and Techniques.* Teacher Ideas Press, 1998.

This writing resource provides information and ideas on what to write about, planning, getting the words to flow on paper, nonfiction and fiction writing workshops, and editing with enthusiasm. The book includes many reproducible checklists and ideas and a very extensive bibliography.

Miller, Wilma H. *Ready-to-Use Activities and Materials for Improving Content Reading Skills.* Center for Applied Research in Education, 1999.

This practical resource for grades 4–12 classroom teachers is packed with hundreds of strategies and reproducible activity sheets for evaluating and improving students' reading, writing, study, and test-taking skills in the content areas (language arts, social studies, science, and mathematics).

Moeller, Marc and Victor. *Middle School English Teachers' Guide to Active Learning.* Eye on Education, 2000.

This book begins with a discussion of two models of teaching: the didactic and the Socratic. It continues with a discussion of active and close reading, the purpose of which is to learn to read to interpret or to pay attention to not only what the author has to say but also how the author says it. What does it say? What does it mean? Is it true? There are three kinds of questions: factual, interpretive, and evaluation. The theory behind active learning is discussed. Sample lessons include questions on various books, including *The Chocolate War, The Giver, Of Mice and Men,* and *The Little Prince.*

Muschla, Gary Robert. *Reading Workshop Survival Kit.* Center for Applied Research in Education, 1997.

Here is everything you need to set up and teach an effective reading workshop where reading is the priority. Part one furnishes guidelines and tools for creating and managing a reading workshop in the classroom. It also offers background information on the process. Part two provides ready-to-use mini lessons with worksheets that focus on reading and related topics, story elements, and a variety of specific reading skills.

Neaman, Mimi and Mary Strong. *Literature Circles: Cooperative Learning for Grades 3–8.* Teacher Ideas Press, 1992.

Step-by-step instructions are furnished on how to teach with literature circles, using thirty popular novels and six picture books. For each title, the authors provide a summary, vocabulary, and many ideas for projects.

Noe, Katherine L. Schlick and Nancy J. Johnson. *Getting Started with Literature Circles.* Christopher-Gordon Publishers, Inc., 1999.

This is from the Bill Harp Professional Teachers Library Series. It is short and concise—filled with lots of practical help for setting up literature circles. The topics include building a framework, classroom climate, structure, good books for literature circles, discussion, response journals, focus lessons, and extension projects.

Raphael, Taffy E., et al. *Book Club: A Literature-Based Curriculum.* Small Planet Communications, 1997.

A video is included with this book. The first portion of the book describes the book club program, including classroom management, assessment, and teaching tips. Next there are lesson plans for eight specific titles, an author study, and five multibook units. There is also a section of additional resources, including reproducible think sheets and assessment forms. This is an excellent resource for starting book discussions as an integral part of a literature program.

Raphael, Taffy E. and Susan I. McMahon. "Book Club: An Alternative Framework for Reading Instruction." *The Reading Teacher.* (October 1994): 102–115.

The book club program "integrates reading, writing, student-led discussion groups, whole-class discussions, and instruction." Many positive changes in student behaviors and abilities were observed as they became more experienced in using the book club program. Earlier conversations were shallow and followed the classroom rules of taking turns rather than authentic conversations. Students learned to develop sequence charts to enhance their understanding, generate various types of questions for discussion, and analyze literary elements. By using this model of reading instruction the authors "learned the importance of integrating reading within the language arts since both discussion and writing promoted students' reading and interpretation of texts."

Rosenblatt, Louise. *The Reader, the Text, the Poem: The Transactional Theory of the Literary Work.* Southern Illinois University Press, 1978.

This is the work in which Louise Rosenblatt discussed the importance of readers connecting with the things they read. This book marks a systematic development in her path-breaking transactional theory of literature. She also shares the definition of the alternate stances: efferent and aesthetic.

Ryder, Randall J. and Michael F. Graves. *Reading and Learning in Content Areas.* Wiley & Sons, 1999.

This college text gives an overview of content-area reading instruction, an outline of the process, and a discussion of the overall literacy of students today. There are chapters on teaching vocabulary, comprehension, critical thinking, writing, cooperative learning, cultural diversity, technology, and assessment—all from the content-area point of view.

Serafini, Frank. *The Reading Workshop: Creating Space for Readers.* Heinemann, 2001.

This book describes daily schedules and an overview of how a reading workshop develops over time. It includes ideas for classroom libraries, museums, shoebox autobiographies, and student discussions and charts, diagrams, and visuals to help get workshops started and to keep them going.

Tiedt, Iris McClellan. *Teaching with Picture Books in the Middle School.* International Reading Association, 2000.

The author introduces adults and students to the numerous possibilities of using picture books in the curriculum. Not only are they fun to read but they also help generate classroom discussion, problem-solving, historical themes, and models for writing.

Towle, Wendy. "The Art of the Reading Workshop," *Educational Leadership* (September 2000): 38–41.

Reading workshop is an approach to reading instruction that provides a framework for teachers to meet the needs of all readers. It allows the teacher to provide one-on-one instructional time with each student every week. Teachers assume that because all the students can read chapter books, all students should read the same book and receive whole class instruction. But this does not allow for each student's strengths and needs. In reading workshop, students spend their time reading and writing to construct meaning. There are five components: teacher sharing time, focus lessons, state of class conference, self-selected reading and responding time, and student-sharing time. The article gives practical ideas for conducting reading workshop, including detailed directions for each of the five components, information on conducting effective individual student conferences, assessment, and record-keeping.

Vacca, Richard T. and Jo Ann L. *Content Area Reading: Literacy and Learning Across the Curriculum*. Longman, 1999.

This college text is an excellent and often-quoted resource for content-area reading. The chapters include teaching and learning with texts, strategy instruction in diverse classrooms, integrating electronic texts and trade books into the curriculum, making authentic assessments, bringing students and texts together, talking and writing to learn, vocabulary and concepts, prior knowledge and interest, study strategies and guides, and growth and reflection in the teaching profession.

Index of Titles and Authors

About the Authors

ELIZABETH KNOWLES, Ed.D, an elementary teacher for 29 years, is currently Director of Staff Development at Pine Crest School in Boca Raton, Florida.

MARTHA SMITH, a media specialist at the same school, has more than 20 years of experience.